Christian Pongratz - Maria Rita Perbellini

Natural Born CAADesigners

Young American Architects

Foreword by Antonino Saggio

D0064445

Birkhäuser – Publishers for Architecture
Basel • Boston • Berlin

Original manuscript in English (excluding foreword)

Foreword translated from Italian into English by David Henderson, Turin

A CIP catalogue record for this book is available from the Library of Congress, Washington D.C., USA.

Deutsche Bibliothek Cataloging-in-Publication Data

Pongratz, Christian:
Natural born CAADesigners: young American architects / Christian Pongratz/Maria Rita Perbellini. Foreword by Antonino Saggio. - Basel ; Boston ; Berlin : Birkhäuser, 2000
   (The IT revolution in architecture)
   ISBN 3-7643-6246-4
   ISBN 0-8176-6246-4

Original edition:
Nati con il computer (Universale di Architettura 71, collana diretta da Bruno Zevi; La Rivoluzione Informatica, sezione a cura di Antonino Saggio).
© 2000 Testo & Immagine, Turin

© 2000 Birkhäuser – Publishers for Architecture, P.O. Box 133, CH-4010 Basel, Switzerland.
Printed on acid-free paper produced of chlorine-free pulp. TCF ∞
Printed in Italy
ISBN 3-7643-6246-4
ISNB 0-8176-6246-4

9 8 7 6 5 4 3 2 1

Contents

To Maria-Rita
To Christian

Our most heartfelt thanks go to Karl Chu, Greg Lynn, Jesse Reiser, Nanako Umemoto, Nonchi Wang, Neil Denari, Elizabeth Diller, Ricardo Scofidio, Winka Dubbeldam, Marcos Novak, Hani Rashid, Lise Anne Couture and Thomas Leeser for their limitless availability and for having supplied us, through interviews, texts, projects and long friendly conversations, the material necessary for the publication of this book. We would also like to thank Luca Galofaro, author of *Digital Eisenman* in this series, and Romi Gandolfi for their unconditional support. This entire book was jointly conceived and written by the two authors. However, the following sections are by Christian Pongratz: chapters 1 and 3, the paragraphs on Chu, Lynn, Denari, Novak and Dubbeldam in chapter 4, and the "Glossary" and "Further Reading" entries relative to the above mentioned chapters and paragraphs. Maria Rita Perbellini was responsible for the following: chapter 2, the paragraphs on Reiser + Umemoto, Nonchi Wang, Diller + Scofidio, Rashid + Couture and Thomas Leeser in chapter 4, the "Biographical Profiles" and the "Further Reading" entries relative to chapter 2 and the above mentioned paragraphs.

Interactivity

Foreword by Antonino Saggio

In 1962 a television came to my house. This was a real event since the waves of information on that black and white screen brought me closer to other children both near and far. At school we could all joke about "Gallina Trik & Trak" or "Giovanna la nonna del corsaro"* and all of us would take a trip together on the flying carpet of Italian children's TV. Perhaps, as they later explained to us, we were being homogenized, but at the time it all seemed great.

Along with the light of day, my son not only saw the light of the television screen, but from his very first moments also had another screen at his disposal. It was in a brown case and was primitive compared to today's standards. Steve and Bill gave birth to it in 1984. I created a hypertext on that first computer so that designs, cartoons and sounds appeared by clicking on "mamma" or "papa". And for hours on end Raffaele interacted with the computer. He was 14 months old.

Today's teenagers play on-line with others in Tokyo or Reykjavik, just as I spoke about the TV characters of Giovanna and Battista the Butler indifferently with either the children of my small village or a large city. If my generation experienced the arrival of television, that of my son was "born" with a TV and computer.

Now, does being "born" when an object or an important technology is already part of the landscape of our life characterize our vision of things and the world? The basic question of this book is precisely that, even if, naturally, more specific. *Natural Born CAAD Designers* studies the architects of the generation that has arrived on the American scene over the last five years and accompanies the reader through the various aspects of that question. For those interested in understanding the architectural imprinting of these new designers, Maria Rita Perbellini and Christian Pongratz have performed a very use-

---

* Trans. note: early Italian television characters.

ful task. They have restricted their selection to ten architecture studios, after having studied many more. They have read the texts, spoken with the architects, analyzed what they have designed (and in some cases built) and offer the reader a unique, new and fresh outlook.

Clouds of Ideas

In situations that are *ongoing*, there are many ideas; situations are fluid and at times confused. Pongratz and Perbellini can not nor do they intend to clarify completely this mass of ideas and experiments. But they do present the architects who characterize them one at a time along with the guiding theories that inspired each one: the research into fluids, anthropomorphic and animated shapes, modal and behavioral states, the search for new amphibious forms, the new virtual dimensions, the search for a complexity drawn directly from contemporary life. One thing becomes very clear; this generation is searching in new territory. We could turn the issue around and imagine our authors on the Florentine scene at the beginning of the 15th century at work on *Naturally Born with Perspective*. Then we would have the ideas of Masaccio and Brunelleschi, Alberti and Donatello, and would hear talk of vanishing points, blueprints, horizons, proportions, of ancient texts and rediscovered heroes of thought such as Plato and Aristotle in the difficult though feasible search for a new, totally human space, totally governed and measured by man and no longer by the Holy Spirit.

This book shows that Karl Chu, Greg Lynn, Reiser + Umemoto, Nonchi Wang, Neil Denari, Diller + Scofidio, Winka Dubbeldam, Marcos Novak, Hani Rashid and Lise Couture, Thomas Leeser and critic/architects such as Stan Allen or Jeffrey Kipnis have set up their research camps in lands faraway from those of the preceding generations. In order to see this, we need only skim through the absolutely indispensable Glossary: What is topological geometry or neo-darwinism? What is an epigenetic landscape or deterministic chaos? The tangle is complex and disconcerting, but it is on these inaccessible lands that the theories of more efficient work will probably emerge.

Aside from the usual *Further Reading* section, the authors have also assembled biographical notes that are a treasure trove of information. Not only bibliographical facts but also Web Sites and e-mail addresses, giving the chance to directly contact that Masaccio or Alberti of tomorrow.

De-formation or In-formation

The book organizes ten articles into a detailed analysis (following the outline indicated by Jeffrey Kipnis in 1993) of the two main trends: the architecture of De-formation and the architecture of In-formation. This is not an insignificant methodological indication. In reality, at least initially, and with all the caution of research in progress, the two main lines of development that those *Natural Born CAAD Designers* are following can be effectively identified. One regards form and therefore the absolutely extraordinary possibility of manipulation and deformation that the computer allows. Manipulating and deforming, as the text clearly shows, not merely for pleasure but rather in search of new substance and new ways of thinking that are embedded in those theories of life, science and thought which seem to be nearer to the present. On the other hand, the rechanneling of concepts from different disciplines towards a common direction is characteristic of each age of change. The fact that art, literature, architecture, design and philosophical, scientific and economic thought are today closer and more interconnected than they have been for decades may be new proof of the Computer Revolution.

The other trend used to group the designers under consideration is that of the architecture of In-formation. Certainly, the first meaning is that of an open form, never concluded, in other words "un-finished", to use a famous, well-known and well-loved term. But the second meaning may also important. The Architecture of Information.

The New Transparency

Information is the greatest commodity of this age. The vegetable we buy at the supermarket is 90% information (research, marketing, distribution). The same, only more so, goes for appliances or automobiles. In addition, more and more people are producing goods that are "pure" information. In other words, information is the key to this age and electronics are its main tool. Now in order to talk about the Architecture of Information, because of the very nature of the subject, we must necessarily take a short step backward.

This book is the sixth in the "IT Revolution" series. The first book contains an afterword called *HyperArchitecture* which lent its title to the entire volume. We must now reconsider this line of thought.

HyperArchitecture means conducting a search for an architecture characteristic of the Information Age. This can not be done without going deep into the heart of the Computer Revolution. This is not so much the bits of information themselves, their immense number and continuing mutability, as much as their capacity to interconnect and interrelate. The structure of the Hypertext is the key. There, the bits of information are connected by channels through which we can freely search, freely find, freely construct our own story.

So the challenge is not only how to create an architecture that is narrative and metaphorical, as is a part of all contemporary architecture, but how architecture itself can be effectively interactive.

But just a moment; the problem here is not of a technical nature. We know that smart houses exist in which the environment changes depending on the situation. There is the "host" scenario in which certain lights are dimmed and doors opened, several sliding walls or double ceilings are moved, a temperature or air flow is created and then the DVD starts up with a certain film or musical selection. Perhaps, and this is already on its way to us with microfibers in wall coverings, the physical characteristics of the walls may also be able to interactively change in grain, porosity and their capacity to absorb sound or color. And the opposite "house with children" scenario could also be obtained in which everything is changed, or even a "sleep" scenario or a thousand others. As in the house of William Gates, we can create a scenario for every situation. Furthermore, the architecture can interactively mutate with the external environment; with the wind, the light, noises, the flow of visitors, and temperature. The real problem, as always, is not of a technical nature, which is easy and almost banal – even if it well deserves our attention and admiration – but rather of an esthetic nature. In other words, how to construct an architecture that would have the "knowledge" to be capable of being interactive, of being able to have structures, spaces and situations that are as navigable and modifiable as a hypertext.

Using steel-reinforced cement in the new architecture of the Twenties did not require in itself a new esthetic. Old buildings could be made with support pillars and beams and then recovered with a coat of stucco following the classic Renaissance perspective. But through a collective effort progressing from the *Glass Pavilion* by Bruno Taut to the *Maison de verre* by Pierre Chareau and passing through Gropius, Mies and Mendelsohn, architects understood that perhaps the transparency permitted by the punctiform structure was the key to a different vision of the world. No more interior-exterior separation, but a freer way of relating to the environment.

Transparency, precisely since it represented the fundamental esthetic of the new architecture, also became the ethic: the willingness to objectively open up toward the new world.

Today we not only have a very powerful method for conceiving, manipulating and building but are also faced with a great, new theme: What is the esthetic sense of interactivity? Will the breakthrough role played by transparency in the new architecture of the Twenties be held today by interactivity? Will the new architecture allow everyone to be both actor and protagonist? Will our children be able to interact not only with the monitor but with the environment and the world and especially with the space of architecture in a new dimension of our being?

We have taken many steps forward from the first book in the Computer Revolution series. New books will fascinate and surprise you because of the small but very vital group of people who are working on this question.

Saggio@axrma.uniroma1.it

Scene of the Crime

MICKEY: You don't understand Wayne. You and I aren't even the same species. I used to be you then I evolved. From where you're standing you're a man. From where I'm standing, you're not even an ape. You're a media person.

WAYNE: Are you done? Let's cut the B.S. and get real. Why this purity you feel about killing? Why for christ's sake?! Why?! Don't lie to me!

MICKEY: I guess Wayne, you got to hold that old shot gun in your hand and it becomes clear like it did for me the first time. I realized my one true calling in life.

WAYNE: What's that?

MICKEY: Shit man, I'm a natural born killer.

(Oliver Stone, *Natural Born Killers*)

1.1 Rethinking Traditional Architectural Assumptions

The implementation of digital techniques indicates another important paradigm shift in architecture after Modernism.

With the introduction of Computer-Aided Design into early conceptual phases within architectural practice through innovative modeling and visualization tools, complex mathematical equations can be used to describe space and develop form. The algorithms of the computational processes allow the visualization of complex organizations and, with the help of design software, the conception of previously un-thinkable, non-orthogonal geometry such as emergent, often unexpected topological forms constituted of multiple different variables, or virtual environments that emerge from *non-linear systems* (see "Glossary"). The computer should not be conceived only as an aid to design but as an evolutionary accelerator and a generative force, applied to complexities associated with built and virtual environments. Used in architectural space perception, the computer enables "a complete overthrow of many traditional and static architectural assumptions, from the typology of organizational structures, to the hierarchical order of planning a structure, ending with the details" (Van Berkel 98)

Virtuality involves the replacement of all existing architectural constants with variables. The computing tool initiates a sudden change in the way of conceiving spatial modalities and allows architecture to overcome its limitations, to supply rules and patterns unknown to its classical language. The machine cannot refer to an existing historical canon. It does not think critically about multiple variables, it does not imply an architectural hierarchical organization: all data is equal.

1.2 From CAAD to CAADesigners

Until recently, the typical use of digital technology in architecture has been limited to enhancing efficiency, productivity, and the visual impact of the work. Computers have been deployed primarily to emulate traditional modes of production; to replicate ink drafting, simulate perspectival views and the experience of walking through a building. Moreover, computer modeling generally tended to occur after a design was substantially completed and only minor modifications were made.

The emphasis on the use of most Computer-Aided Design Systems has been on the detailed description and modeling of single design ideas rather than on the exploration of multiple alternatives. If we use the computer unimaginatively in the design process, we will not exploit the full capability of any available program. As a result of the latest technology used in innovative practices, however, new fluid models, modifiable and evanescent forms are emerging that no longer conform to anachronistic notions of space as finite and static.

Computer *simulation* (see "Glossary") enables architecture to invest in potentialities such as what Leibniz delineated as the combinatorial and interactive dynamic system*.

---

* G. Wilheim Leibniz (Leipzig 1646–1716) studies, later but independently from Newton, the mathematical principles of infinitesimal calculus and proposes the metaphysical theory that we live in "the best of all possible worlds". The universalistic requirement of his philosophy is expressed in the unitary, but also pluralistic, research of the world, in which the different forms of man's knowledge and experience will find harmony, without

THE ARTISTRY OF COMPUTATION

The current technical research is able to copy nature in order to create artificial ontological processes, where cell division and development incorporate autonomous forces of phylogenetic mutation, recombination and selection.

loosing their specificity. His logic consists of the reduction of all concepts to simple elements; to each of them is given a numeric symbol; after we have found the combination rules between the symbols, it will be possible to express every discourse as a mathematical calculus, and through new combinations and new calculus, we will discover new truths (*De Arte Combinatoria*, 1672).

The possibility of an "imaginative use" of digital techniques means compressing evolutionary space and time so that hybrid, interconnected architectural spatialities are able to develop.

The Computer, as a source of inspiration, is the device with the power and the speed to go beyond the limits of our perceptions.

1.3 Crossing Disciplines

In order to understand some of the motivating forces behind the innovative architectural approaches we will examine, we have to look at contemporary scientific research in disciplines such as, among others, biology and physics that are interested in the reconstruction and simulation of life processes and their micro-organizations.

Information exchanges on any level induce relationships sensitive to external influences and generate mutations. Various explorations into complex life structures – and their inner, spontaneously animated processes and self-organizing systems – are supported by scientific experiments that predominantly deal with geometry. Similar mapped models and their implementation technically then transform what constitutes the molecular and material structures of digital machines, including computers, into higher levels of organizations.

Inspired by the principles of evolution and biological development, a new generation of computer hardware is being designed. The chips will be adaptable, self-regenerating and self-replicating. This provides the basis for the use of constantly improving architectural modeling systems, which forces an advanced understanding of geometry through fast, simulated, experimental and intuitional methodologies.

Also other domains of research of unfolding evolution, which integrate our whole environment into an advanced electronic infrastructure, use data from various disciplines.

Therefore, this combination will ultimately modify all our thought and perception, where we will have to interact seamlessly through all kinds of multidimensional responsive interfaces.

1.4 Fluid, Seamless Integration

A great part of our physical environment and existence is already undergoing an epochal transformation from a solid to a liquid state on many levels of technological evolution. Especially important is the global communication of all kinds of machines, of digital and electronic systems through networks. Rapidly increasing knowledge thus leads to the creation, engineering and reproduction of differentiated matter, where existing analog parts are gradually but without exception transformed into digital modules. Ultimately, all man-machine interfaces of hardware will be adequately infinitely machined so any interactivity results in a smooth transmission of visual, sound and tactile sensations. This process will continue, however, beyond the current level of TV, video, cellular-phones and computers, incorporating interconnected surfaces of text, music and other kinds of data. The surrounding sensorium will penetrate the phenomenological tissue of our nervous system to the extent that we will interact unconsciously and fluidly. Their behavioral properties and molecular organizational capacities, will provide an intellectual and sensual presence which renders space and its perception as being liquefied.

The interrelation of and between the building's exterior skin and its interior usage will also be smooth and multidimensional, as they are able to alter their properties in response to contextual changes or movements. Sanford Kwinter calls this scaleless integration of systems, with architectural and material articulations that are electro-material environments, a world of multilevel flows of complex inter-penctrations of technical, architectural, biological and social structures, seamlessly embodied into a fluid or near liquid geometry in real time.

2. The Young American Architects

2.1 Sons without Fathers

We will seek to reexamine architecture's place within cultural practices, within the realms of technological innovation, media and telecommunications. The immediate dissemination of information through a global computer network is producing an impact never experienced before. Linear time has been absorbed by technology that has introduced the simultaneity and the instantaneousness of the digital response. New investigations traverse fluctuating territories that define the spatiality of the information age, in which borders become blurred, in a revised perception of space, time and meaning. How to redefine architecture in an information society is the challenge for the new generation, which has to reinvent the whole discipline, to overcome its fixed norms and to respond with a reconceptualization of its interiority, opening outward to other disciplines.

In this sense, the search is on for a more flexible and dynamic architecture, where conventions of the past have little meaning. The digital age, global economies, biotechnology, information as commodity stage a revolt. As Hani Rashid states, through his direct involvement, this is the first generation of architects that is not working under the burden of Modernism. They are slightly freer of the responsibility to take on Modern Architecture than their predecessors; they are bored with Modernism in all of its reconstructions and quotations. Architects such as Gehry, Eisenman, Koolhaas, like many others, have worked under the extremely powerful influence and inherited the consciousness of demigods like Mies van der Rohe, Le Corbusier and Aalto, that preceded them. These heroes of Modernism are no longer present; the new architects are working on different terrain where ever-expanding thresholds of speed, efficiency and meaning are changing our comprehension of the city space. It is now possible to develop a certain level of complexity in design, to explore geometries or modalities that were previously impossible to pursue, and realistically experience an unbuilt space.

Within the selection of young Americans, we have included a diversified group of professionals, around forty years old, operating in different contexts and involved in a computerized practice of architecture. They grew up with the invention of

FROM COLLAGE TO *MORPHING*

At the end of the twenties Mies van der Rohe used photomontage to render the contrast between his pure, "alien" tectonic form and its surrounding nineteenth-century buildings facing busy metropolitan streets. Stuttgart Bank Competition, 1928. (The picture is from Hilberseimer 84).

Contemporary examples of morphing effects of used by Hollywood film industry are movies such as Terminator II. *The liquid mercury man can become or disappear into any form through smooth morphological transformation.*

the PC, Internet, with the dissemination of information technologies, cellular telephones and satellite-based telecommunication, videoconferencing and virtual images, home shopping networks and pervasive media-entities. Accordingly, constant ubiquity and interactivity opens the way for architects to operate in new territories, in a new built environment within the folds of information space.

By contrast, in the early 20th century, the Modernist avantgarde lodged their creative energy within the metropolis. The modern city was a place of resistance and at the same time was an active subject, the locus of collision or juxtaposition. 16 Mies' projects were rendered with the technique of collage where the pure geometry of the new building declares its difference with its surrounding.

What is changing is the relation to a new urban context, which does not contain the same resistance. Recent forms of social transformations, continuous re-inventions and unknown possibilities are now the places in the non-place of contemporary urban life.

> Collages have succumbed to techniques such as *morphing*, an operation far more like what Deleuze and Guattari discuss in their description of becoming: in their jargon, the elements that temporarily define an entity, "deterritorialize" and "reterritorialize" elsewhere, forming other temporary entities. (M. Novak, *Trans urban optimism*)

Peter Eisenman's Aronoff Center, Frank Gehry's Guggenheim Museum and Daniel Libeskind's Jewish Extension to the Berlin Museum started to modify the language, which is now consciously re-written within new paradigms by the successive young generation. There is a shift from representation to a strong interest in organization and form, in terms of what it is possible to produce in the design process as a result of architectural implications in the virtual realm. Nevertheless, Peter Eisenman, with the innovative vigor of his forms and methods, is one of the most important theoretical figures for young architects, students, and intellectuals of different backgrounds.

Still the new architect needs to escape from an oedipal relationship. It doesn't matter who the father is.

> Architecture does not get any better. Le Corbusier is just different from Palladio, Serlio, Piranesi, Giulio Romano, or anybody with a discourse. It is changing, it is responding to different social and cultural conditions. (Eisenman, *AA Files 25*)

2.2 Tools and Effects

Most of the architects we considered installed the first machine at least 10 years ago, others more recently, within the last 4 or 5 years. They use various architectural design software packages, today highly malleable, easier to learn and to program, such as Microstation, AutoCAD and ArchiCAD.

Some prefer to work with Form Z, Softimage or 3D Studio for modeling and rendering, or advanced animation and industrial design software such as Alias and Maya for complex modeling tasks. Photoshop and Freehand are also popular for producing representations.

Each upgrade and new software product used in work is even more versatile. Yet, the computer is not the sole reliable generator of a project. There are more inputs in the design process than just the pure electronic solution. With a simply pragmatic approach, physical models are still produced (for example: laser-cut laminated objects), as well as sketches, often used to visualize the first notional, organizational idea. In the case of a more complex structural level, the computer is involved from the beginning.

However, the tool that operates best will be chosen, the one most effective in solving the problem immediately. There is a new materialistic view of computation where one can say that some real manual models are actually also computational. The reason is that computer drawings need to be tested repeatedly in a real environment, especially if the geometry represents a complex space frame that will be built. The result is a real model that is a physical system of computation. There is an exciting dance back and forth between modeling geometry on the computer and its translation into a real product. The analog model, although at times simply repeating the digital one, is useful as it remains present after the power is shut down. Therefore, its life is continuous and seamless and can provide food for thought, in a process of producing something that is continually modifiable, changeable, and evolvable.

2.3 Influences without Geography

The young architects we selected belong to two groups:
– architects who were born, educated, live, work and teach in the USA (East Coast, West Coast), but with experience of education-work in Europe or Asia;
– architects educated in Europe or Asia until undergraduate degree; some of them received a Master's degree in architecture from an American university, and have had experience of living-working-teaching in the USA over the last ten years.

What seems to be significant is the presence of two identities facing two situations:
– born in the USA and seeing European-Asian experience as a moment of intellectual exchange, as the expression of a social and ethical discourse;
– born in Europe or Asia and choosing the USA as a place to find a conscience in architecture, a place of philosophical challenge, a new terrain of experimentation.

This cursory introduction of several presences on the "scene of the crime" is necessary because it introduces the question of cultural, geographical and local influences in architecture.

Key concepts like globalization, information and telecommunications all suggest that place no longer matters. Hence, a multiplicity of components, activities and culturally diversified situations are present in the new transnational and re-territorialized culture. The neutralization of distance through telematics has its correlate in new types of structures constituted as cyberspaces.

We have chosen to explore the work of young architects

RAPID PROTOTYPING

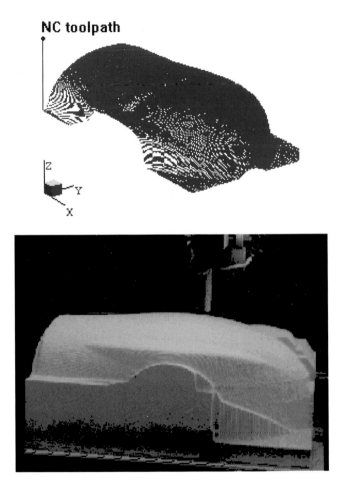

Top: DeskProto window showing part of the NC toolpath (the first layer). Bottom: The actual milling of the prototype, on a three axis Deckel machine. Delft Spline Systems (calculation of the NC milling paths). Machines such as a computer numerically controlled (CNC) mill can cut the digital 3D-model out of polymer or wax substances. Any resulting plastic mold is then used to create, for example, concrete façade elements or space frames.

based in large cities such as New York and Los Angeles, strategic places that concentrate new advanced information flows and condense the diversity and multiplicity of other cultures and identities. Without a doubt, the energy, the vertical tension and the sense of compression typical of New York provokes a different impact than the endless horizontal panorama of Los Angeles.

Facing the complexity of urban phenomena, the new architects nevertheless prefer to respond to it critically. Given the multiformity of changes in the social and political space of the city, not just in America, but everywhere, it is important to acknowledge the revolutionary relationship between architecture as the discipline that regulates stable, constructible urban and territorial hierarchies and the consequences of a limitless, variable dimensional cyberspace, interacting with technologies of computational reality.

Notions of time, speed, movement, flows, displacement, transit, noise and liquidity are just some of the influences that become the common elements of the training of the architect of the future, all reflecting activities, situations and needs more than geographic implications. In addition, the urban context is a communal experience of the city, not only as a constructed environment but also as an event that includes media, which again does not respect the traditional notion of boundary or any spatial limitation.

The type of territory represented by major cities and their suburbs or communities has dissolved. There is a trend to go beyond any sign of locality, to feel oneself part of somewhere unbounded, working without borders. Likewise, the new terrain is an unbounded area of interdisciplinary research from philosophy to science. As Stan Allen indicated, it is crucial to resist location and specialization and to maintain the possibility of working fluidly. Expressing his position, he declares:

> I am more interested in the urban effects of new technologies, the new patterns of life and work made possible by technology, the unprecedented reconfigurations of the political spaces of the city, than

in abstract speculations about new constitutions of reality suggested by technological advances. (Allen 1993)

2.4 The Breeding Ground

In America, a high percentage of people start to teach after graduation, often without any previous practical experience. Columbia, Princeton, Cooper Union (just to mention some of the East coast campuses) or UCLA, SCI-Arc (West coast), are places of continuous inspiration where young architects have the opportunity, in teaching, to develop theoretical ideas in relation to computer-aided technology, applied later to their work. Columbia University, for example, called one recent program "Paperless Studio" because all the design phases in the third-year digital/media architecture courses are inevitably done on computers, with 33 Power Macintosh and Silicon Graphics workstations.

Yet, there is always the danger in using these digital tools of producing aggregations that are merely graphical rather than architectural. In educational practice, these new teacher-architects set rules to respect, as well as certain directions to follow. They always include exercises in measurable spaces and this tendency is related to the need to keep the graphical aspect of the image under control. In his class, Jesse Reiser tries to deal mainly with space in scale, avoiding perspectives. He keeps the student's attention on traditional plans, sections, and elevations. Greg Lynn attempts to use the computer in school less in the way a renderer does and more as a form and pattern generator. It is important not to lose control, especially with software like Alias which was designed mainly for Hollywood cartoons and has recently been applied in the automobile industry. Lynn has pointed out that there is an aesthetic value in this software. Everything gets deformed. Design shifts a little bit; it is a kind of formative design rather than traditional design. Hani Rashid, merely in seeing his students' excitement, desire and drive to probe electronic and digital realms, to look for new space, is sure that they grasp a glimpse of the future.

3. Premeditation

3.1 An "Intermedial" Architecture

The Newtonian paradigm of linear sciences is currently complemented by the sciences of complexity which add, among others, non-linear dynamics, fractals and self-organizing systems. As a result, the exploration of non-linear structures, forms, shapes and geometries in architecture advances without reference to Euclidean (see "Glossary") or Cartesian geometry. Additionally, there is a conviction that it is necessary to exploit not only scientific research into micro-organisms but also the philosophical discourse that deals with significant contemporary cultural changes.

Derridian post-structuralist thought brought us into the era of post-modern architecture, questioned the logocentrism of the discipline and led to the deconstructivist movement. A successive shift from language/text-oriented philosophy and its influence on the main Neo-Avantgardists (such as Eisenman, Tschumi and others) to the substance-oriented discourse of Gilles Deleuze and Félix Guattari, reintroduced a material and structural consciousness into architecture.

Moreover, architecture is entering an age of fluidity that expresses and creates new modalities, opening up possible worlds organized in different, simultaneous configurations, in hybrid spatialities. Optical phenomena and radical shifts in visuality, particularly manifest through media and digital technologies, are impacting on the city space in unpredictable ways. The urban realm is construed as surveillance, simulation, distraction and a relentless proliferation of information which is reshaping the way we perceive, inhabit and utilize cities. As a consequence, the multiplicity of goals and directions of the vast field of young American post-avantgarde exploration cannot be reduced to styles and languages in the traditional sense of architecture. Yet, the argument of the next millennium may still hinge on form versus formlessness or what Jeff Kipnis calls "deformation" versus "information".

In other words, the notion of an "intermedial architecture" which is intelligent, interactive and virtual in its organization,

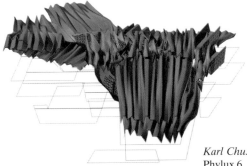

Karl Chu. From Phylux *series:* Phylux 6

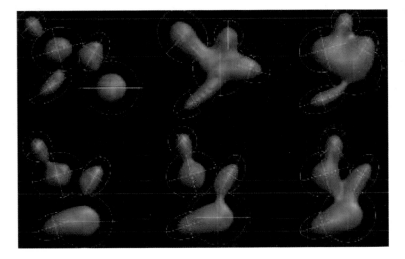

This image explains the basic concept of the "blob". Specifically located nodes within a field start to interact with each other, according to their zones of assigned gravitational force, which can be seen as a sphere of influence. The computer calculates a condition of balance of all nodes, a highly complex process with an infinite number of possible variations. Step by step, the nodes grow and fuse into a new node with combined influence. This process continues until growth leads to a state of equilibrium. During the growth simulation, the weight of the gravity forces can be manipulated

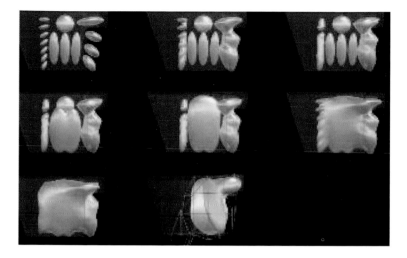

and allows interactively directing the result. This strategy of the "blob" as explained above, is used to generate a single volume resulting from the growth and fusion process of separate programmatic nodes at the beginning. What starts as a collection of single rooms(nodes), ends as a single surface, which incorporates the entire program. Korean Presbyterian Church of New York, 1995 (built).

Design team*: Douglas Garofalo Architects in Chicago, Illinois; Michael McInturf Architects in Cincinnati, Ohio and Greg Lynn FORM in Venice, California.*

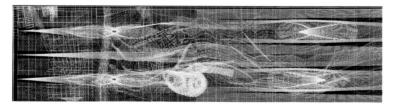

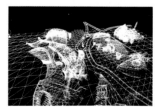

Above: topological geometries of roof and floor patterns. Reiser+Umemoto, Kansai Library, Japan (competition entry, 1996). Left: Wireframe. Nonchi Wang, The Service Area of the Logistic Activity Zone of the Port of Barcelona - ZAL, (competition entry, 1996).

develops along two major trajectories. First, as Andrew Benjamin termed it, there is the problem of formalism, the formal innovation that emerges through progress in science and computational technology. Here, the instrument chosen to generate the design, or specific characteristics in the generative process may lead to smooth and malleable topological systems with an emphasis on formal assembly.

However, it is the organizational structure and the inherent interaction between different media that accelerates the potential for a differentiated reality to emerge.

Secondly, another line of current research stems from a non-conventional "otherness" that redefines space through the interface between architecture and media. However, this includes a heterogeneous group of approaches. These represent a search into vibrant hypermedia or into virtual tectonics in cyberspace, into virtual textures, into our live-ness or into the flatness of collective code-systems; all different states of a common dynamic convergence whose technological manifestations redefine the interaction of architecture and the user through the propagation of information flows. The resulting condition is a fluid, flexible and dynamic architectural space that potentially supersedes reality. The limited duration in time and the tendency to dematerialize emerging structures are a result of a cross-penetration of multiple streams of information, energy and movement, and dominate a redefined space, consisting of variables and virtual agents.

24-25 3.2 Topological Surfaces (De-formation)

Pioneering models of flexibility have been introduced into contemporary architecture. Their progressive evolution through dynamic methodologies in computer design have led to a new plasticity in the exploration of form, replacing familiar codes with more stimulating approaches. Deleuze's original concept of the "fold" has now progressed through continuous, endless transformations into the forms of a curved landscaped.

The predominant aspect of the current formal issue is the introduction of *soft topological systems* (see "Glossary", *Topological Geometry*). The strategies used are capable of computer-generating temporal events within architectural surfaces and their overall topological continuity. However, it is the emerging geometries that allow the incorporation of cultural and contextual differences as contingent influences within architectural form.

The characteristics of tension and deformation in the resulting continuous curvilinear soft systems transform existing spatial qualities through smooth affiliations with their environment. Relationships with the site appear that are undetermined and unexpected since they do not emphasize a prevailing architectural language, typology or material. Instead, as Kipnis argues, they amplify characteristics hidden in the site and generate a coherent incongruity.

To better understand the process, one has to visualize the topological surface and imagine it behaving like a natural landscape, following a discontinuous logic and capable of assimilating and recording the inflections of virtual forces as a slow undulation of its shape in time. Therefore the design process in general is often involved with a priori flexible "bodies" involved in an infinite sensory interaction with their external physical conditions. The most important effect is a fluid variation of difference between the constituting forms. The overall shape is flexible or elastic, "and still has coherent parts that form a fold such that they are not split up into fragments of fragments, but are rather infinitely divided into smaller and smaller folds that always retain a certain cohesion (Gilles Deleuze, *The Fold*).

Therefore, this smooth and continuous mixture can not be reduced into its component parts since it is not a homogeneous form and appears rather as one aggregate. It produces an architectural form that has the potential of being soft, flexibly curved, shaped by external influences and capable of reacting with the strategies and sensibilities of a pliant system. The computational process, made dynamic especially by techniques such as animation, puts a strategy into play that resembles the natural evolutionary process of genetic selection and mutation. Considering certain contextual forces and deciding about their interrelation is an input that is more or less arbitrary

IN-FORMATION ARCHITECTURE

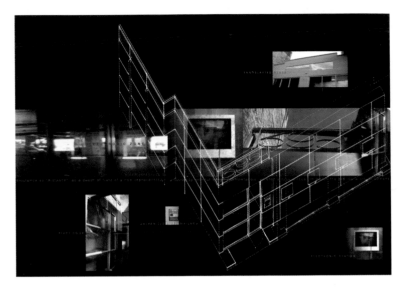

Winka Dubbeldam, Christine Rose, *Mixed-Media Art Gallery, New York City, 1994.*

Rashid + Couture (Asymptote Architecture), Iscape.

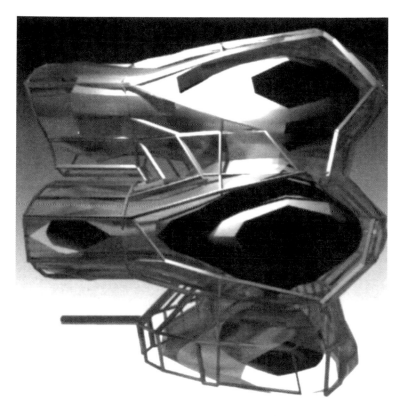

Marcos Novak, Transweb, *1997.*

and primary, but also intuitive and with a sense of the virtuality of the process. Every change or differentiation is a result of the combination of virtual forces selected and exerted on given forms. However, the *modus operandi* set in motion often produces chance effects through certain still undetermined factors.

In Brian Massumi's interpretation, the virtual gives form, but has none itself. Form itself is a derivative of a movement that continues on beyond. This means, that the virtuality of form exceeds its actuality.

The proliferation of forms in this field of exploration and

experimentation emerges from a process that is not purely autonomous and sometimes even unpredictable, but one that requires certain critical decisions of selection. The variation is the growing virtual nature of the objects. It may give a different organization of the limits of the program in order to reach certain desired results. This implies that, for any conceived prototype, its elastic shape represents a visual trace or residue of the process of change and its incorporated forces. Eventually, the final selected prototype is an example of an organized whole of suitable characteristics perfectly adapted to preset parameters.

28-29 3.3 Hypersurfaces

An ever growing number of architects are showing interest in the continually accelerating cycles of consumer culture and the omnipresence of information flows. Freed from the formal extravagance of the complex or the grandiose gesture, they are instead intrigued by the close exploration of media culture and technology. They take inspiration from contemporary culture's proliferation of images through graphic language and telematic visual expressions. There is therefore a questioning of the role of contemporary architecture in the information age since semiotic mutations more than ever challenge architecture in its traditional role of representation. The icons of Modernism, such as "form-follows function" which represents architecture's instrumentality, are ineffective against current media production and unarmed when faced with means of communication capable of clubbing one senseless.

In this sense, some approaches question traditional architectural hierarchies along with its common assumptions but without the escape to pure formal emphasis. There is an effort to overcome the form based solely on architecture's interiority, separated from symbol and meaning.

Stephen Perrella introduced the term "pixel architecture" to describe practices that transform architectural surfaces and dissolve form within a show of images, such as digital electronic signs for example. This type of operation creates new material and spatial designs, neutralizing the form in its modernistic values. Architecture is redefined by drawing from the legacy of media technology and its abundance of figures. Their evocation of information space challenges capitalistic representation systems, and incorporates interactive information play within real and virtual surfaces of architecture. The visual layering of programmed and technological effects refers back to the concepts of Kipnis such as "information architecture" (see "Further reading", 3.1 "Inter-medial Architecture") or "blankness", to differentiate modernist ideals of formal abstraction from generating unplanned affiliations. This means suppressing any formal or figural reference – a kind of *tabula rasa* – and delineates a shift from "free-façade" to "free-massing".

An emerging insight into virtual configurations of space propels this experimental architecture. It engages and creates adaptive and tactile physical environments, which surround and envelope our physical and conceptual bodies. This will result in a seamless integration of information, technology and users, generating an endlessly infinite sensitive surface. Architecture - and its cohesive elements identified within sensitive shells, together with an inner interactivity of parts, where every one forms the machine of a machine - mimics an infinitely endless soft system. It is the liquefaction of the posturban environment.

4. Differences

Our selection and order of the architects does not refer to any traditional categories. It neither corresponds to original concepts referring to a certain style, nor is the embodiment of an iconography such as visual design and its manifestation and materialization in a constructed form. The choice of categorizing certain approaches into *de-formation* or *in-formation* architecture is a method that, while assisting the reader in the field of objectives, should still preserve the individual expression shown by the single designers which differentiates their own work.

MODAL SPACE: KARL CHU

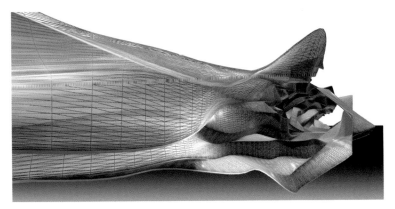

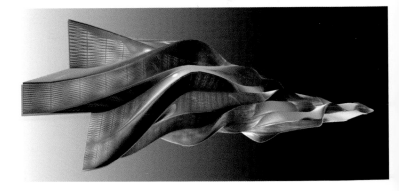

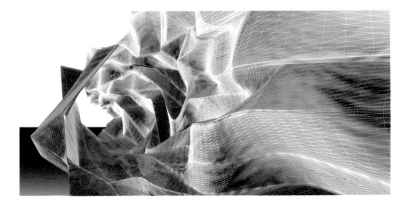

Genetic space is a tapping into the creative logic of evolutionary systems where the possibility for recursive generation of intelligible structures, as expressions of machinic orality, is folded into complex variables and functions. Karl Chu (X Kavya), Phylox *series.*

Page 32, from top to bottom: Phylox 1, Phylox 3, Phylox 5. *This page:* Phylox 4, Phylox 6.

4.1 De-formation Architecture

Rejecting Cartesian geometry, Karl Chu is primarily concerned with metaphysics and specifically ontology implemented through theoretical computation and applied to architectural design as complex adaptive systems. Yet, he does not follow pure rationalistic tendencies but rather a cosmic and pluralistic concept of reason which refers to the notion of "Monadology" as defined by Leibniz in 1714. The German philosopher-mathematician sustained that the universe is made up of living "monads", or simple and individual substances, centers of power and activity, at the same time spiritual and also the foundation of corporeal reality, infinite in their variety. Each monad is potentially the representation not just of itself, but also of the whole universe. The agreement between monads – for a given modification into a certain reality which corresponds to a given modification into another reality – is prearranged according to a preestablished harmony.

This concept recognizes the method of combination as a basic alternative for the differentiation of identity. However, instead of proceeding through a classical analysis of system constituents or their reduction, it permits an evolutionary differentiation. This kind of evolution and its implied complexity is governed by an internal logic of algorithmic and experimental mathematical reality. It indicates a shift to the continuous substance of relations as suggested in differential calculus and the equations of Leibniz.

The current information paradigm leads to the argument that even natural processes are some kind of computation. In the current emerging virtual worlds, the capacity of aggregations of abstract machines leads to the co-evolution of hyperstructures as higher forms of self-organization. The same informational-theoretical origin applied to contemporary research in Artificial Life leads to the innovative computations of Cellular Automata (CA) and Genetic Algorithms (GAs).

Chu's architectural investigations at the edge of chaos, are applications of the dynamic behavior systems of CA/GAs into time-based design strategies. It is a "machinic" concept from which a creative modeling of genetic structures is stimulated through evolutionary systems. These are generative systems that are dynamic organizations in the sense that they are self-modifying and organizing, with an infinite potential for differentiation.

The intelligible structures, calculable relationships and possible morphogenetic forms between them led Chu to the notion of *modal space*, where the category of the possible has a systematic logic of embodiment. In other words, a logic of instrumental "build-ability" is experienced in the modeling of physical systems, where information dynamically propels a methodology of construction connected to generative systems.

Eventually the realm of *virtual reality* (see "Glossary") will change current notions of cost or energy faced with the effects of the algorithmic compression of enormous amounts of information or the complexity of exchange and interaction of information systems.

The following is Chu's unpublished text, related to the conceptual evolution of his work presented in this publication:

> *The Caesura of the Turing* dimension*
>
> If tragedy, or a certain philosophical interpretation of tragedy, is the origin and active matrix of speculative thought in general, and dialectical thought in particular, the emerging phenomena that is about to explode into the virtual universe of possible worlds will not escape the resonance of the tragic effect that accompanies and haunts speculative endeavors. The recurrence of tragedy has been in the making for the last two thousand years beginning with Euclid's axiomatic treatment of geometry to Russel's and Whitehead's *Principia Mathematica*. It is a consequence of the manifest destiny of instrumental reason that finds

---

* Alan Turing (London 1912–1954) was a pioneer in computer calculations. During the Second World War, with his London team, he built a machine called *Colossus*, one of the first completely electronic digital computers, that was used to interpret coded German radio messages. He also theorized an ideal machine (the Universal Turing Machine, mentioned by Karl Chu in this text) that clarified the concept of computability and defined a calculation model essential for the construction of machines capable of solving any solvable problem.

MODAL SPACE: K. CHU

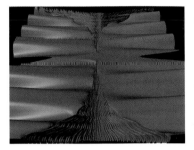

Karl Chu, Phylux, Blue Series.

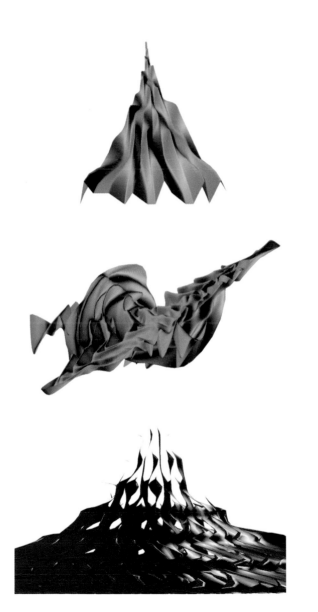

Top and meadow: Phylux, Beige Series. *Bottom:* Red Series.

concrete expression in the Universal Turing Machine (UTM)*. In its current resurgence, the subject is no longer the sole locus of the tragic effect which has already begun to permeate across the virtual surface of the plane of immanence re-defined and framed by the Universal Turing Machine. This tragic dimension is the scene of a transfusion where the Subject of speculative Idealism finds him/herself immersed into the manifold cockpit of the Universal Turing Surface now being engendered by the Universal Turing Machine. It is a trajectory that merges with the instrumental medium by steering it according to the infinite movements of thought and lines of flight in order to overcome the fabric of mimetology brought on by the machine of the *double bind*. It is a catharsis, both, of the subject and of the medium, the Universal Turing Surface that insinuates the substance of Aristotelian *mimesis* as a mode of *poiesis*, or *mimesis* in the sense of mimetism or imitation. It is this onto-theological aspiration behind every metaphysical desire that induces a philosophy of the tragic effect by situating the subject in an in-between space of melancholy, or *metaxy*, to use Plato's designation, which is at once the nearest and yet the farthest from absolute fulfillment. In the "brave new world" that is unfolding, the horizons of the tragic effect will no doubt resonate on the contours of the Universal Turing Surface. The Turing dimension is the one-dimensional universe of monadic states derived from the law of the series. Together with the arrow of time, the Turing dimension establishes the plane of reference necessary for the Universal Turing Surface to appear. The UTM is a diagrammatic machine that rolls and unrolls the Universal Turing Surface into architecture of manifolds. Herein lies the supreme irony of a gnostic quest that may well be usurped by the very instrument that promises to deliver. The ambition of the Universal Turing Surface is to rise to the level expressive of an oracle by encapsulating Leibniz's notion of the Principle of Sufficient Reason. It attempts at a formal representation of the universe as a pre-established harmony of coordinated monads to form a *plenum*. However, the internal principle contained within each computational monad is dependent on the universe of computable functions drawn from the universe of mathematics that has proven to be irreducibly random and incomplete. As a consequence, any algorithmic compression of a theory of everything that embodies the Principle of Sufficient Reason can only occur, if it occurs at all, on a time scale that is exponentially beyond many life times of the universe. The drama of the incomplete thus haunts the dimension of the tragic effect induced by the infinite expanse of the Universal Turing Surface. The Surface is ingrained with gaps, holes and vortices amidst the desert ocean teeming with infozoic (the artificial life of digital monads) life forms. The caesura enters into these gaps to sustain a pause or the empty moment, the absence of moment that, if luck is with it, may allow for the intrusion of the prophetic word. Let it suffice for now to say that, the Turing dimension is an infinite line interspersed with dimensions of the tragic effect and the Universal Turing Surface is the instrumental substance that exfoliates into a topo-dramatology of the virtual cockpit infused with an ambivalent mixture or cyclothmic oscillation of exultation and despair. It is at once a tragic comedy and a machinic philosophy of the tragic effect that is, above all else, an onto-organology – a self-synthesized organ of a self-synthesized information system that aspires to a strange form of spiritual life on the surface of demiurgic space. (Karl S. Chu, *X Kavya*, Los Angeles, March, 1999).

ANIMATE FORM: *Greg Lynn (Form)*
Because of his interest in morphology, geometry and form in general, supported through inspiration from other disciplines more advanced in these fields, he named his office literally *Form*.
Lynn agrees with the neo-avantgarde that architecture has to engender contemporary cultural and social differences as well as the potential external contradictions and incongruities of building and context. Yet the chosen strategy is a smoothing of these dissimilar external constraints and forces into a continuum with fluctuations, that softly incorporates these external differences.
The instrumentality of Lynn's techniques is predominantly supported through software tools that originate from the special effects and animation industry. Their implementation into his time and motion based methods produces a dynamic and flexible architecture through an animated design process. Yet, he argues that one cannot rely on the control of the computer, but must understand the conceptual potentialities of this medium to employ it schematically and with systematic human intuition.

ANIMATE FORM : GREG LYNN

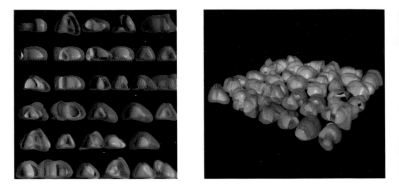

Greg Lynn (Form), Embriological Housing, *Study-project, 1998. Left: One variation of the surface showing the budding and elaboration of the surface in specific regions.*

This study includes a strategy of opening the surface without the punching or cutting of windows. Instead, openings are either "torn" generating a series of "shredded openings" in the surface, or alternatively the surface is "offset" generating a series of "louvered openings" in the surface. Right: the surface envelopes were connected with a landscape so that any alteration in the object was transmitted onto a ground surface. For instance, a dent or concavity in the envelope generates a lift or plateau in the ground. In this way a deformation in the object has a corresponding effect on the field around it, facilitating openings, views and circulation on a potential site.

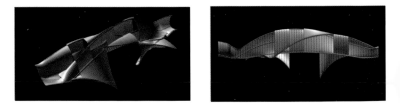

Greg Lynn (Form), Triple Bridge Gateway, Port Authority Bus Terminal, New York City, New York (competition, 1995). Left: camera-view, right: front view.

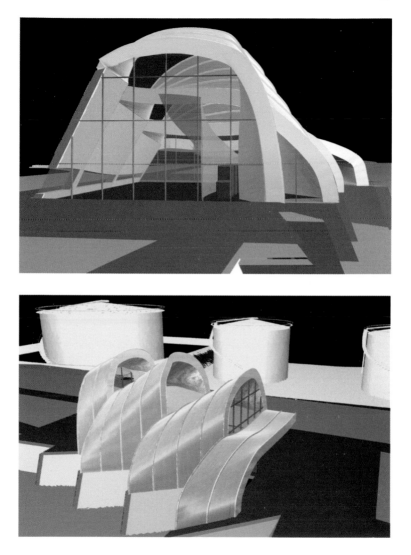

H2 House, Hydrogen House for the OMV corporation, Vienna, Austria (commissioned 1996). Above: front view, below: west view.

Project team: *Michael McInturf Architects in Cincinnati, Ohio; Martin Treberspurg Architects in Vienna, Austria and Greg Lynn Form in Venice, California.*

ANIMATE FORM : GREG LYNN

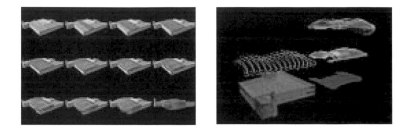

Korean Presbyterian Church of New York (commissioned 1995, under construction). Left: instead of circular arranged nodes, a parallel alignment is chosen and allows a different manipulation of the growth and fusion process. The shape of the single volume is then arrested after the separate nodes reach their equilibrium. Right: explosion rendering showing the existing factory, rib-like structural tubes and the connecting surfaces inside and for the envelope.

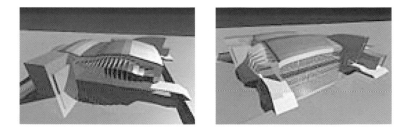

Left: perspective aerial view from the north showing the significant staircase with the exterior metal roof enclosure with a very dense rhythm of metal panels. On the left showing the extending block for the rehearsal spaces. The roof skin is proposed as a metal surface with smooth edges connecting down to the vertical walls. Right: perspective aerial view from the west showing the main elevation and both main entry structures, flanking the curtain wall of the sanctuary space.

West elevation showing the second entry tube in progress.

Left: perspective aereal view of large procession staircase. Above: grand view of sanctuary space with mezzanine balcony seating on the left.

Design team: *Douglas Garofalo Architects in Chicago, Illinois, Michael McInturf Architects in Cincinnati, Ohio and Greg Lynn Form in Venice, California.*

ARCHITECTURE OF THE INCOMPLETE: REISER + UMEMOTO (RUR ARCHI-
TECTURE)

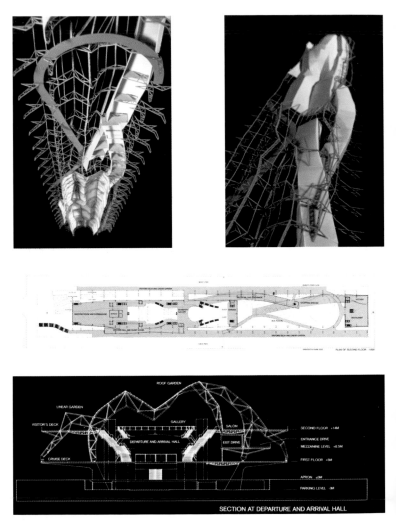

*Yokohama Port Terminal, Japan, Tokyo Bay (competition entry, 1994). Above
left: detail of main path; above right: detail of roof program; middle: plan, second
floor; below: section at departure and arrival hall.*

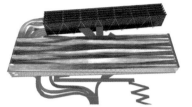

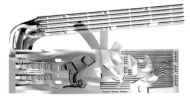

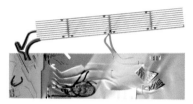

Kansai Library, Japan (competition entry, 1996).From above: roof plan, second floor plate, first floor plate.

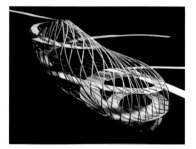

Middle: left, interior view; right, front elevation. Below: left, structural diagram; right, geodetic store.

Central to his dynamic design method under development is the shift from determinism to *directed indeterminacy* (see "Glossary", *Deterministic Chaos*). This can be understood by the mutual presence of two fundamental characteristics: first the employment of a process driven design methodology in an experimental non-linear mode of time and parameters. Second, the necessity for the (abstract animated) systems of organization to be guided in their sometimes unpredictable transformation, mutation and growth. Otherwise, in a kind of "hyper-functional Darwinism", computational intelligence will run evolutionary models through undecidable morpho-genetic iterations.

It is an experiment of unfolding deformations in various ways, such as bending or twisting while still presenting a large continuous surface, achieved through the advancement of topological geometries.

40 The paneled surface in the *Embriological Housing* project utilizes sets of controlling points in order to network groups of panels in such a way that any single inflection results in a mutation of every other panel.

Computer Animation and its time-based milieu changes the way shapes and volumes are conceived, from points within Cartesian space to vectors of transformation describing topological surfaces. A characteristic surface curvilinearity is the effect of contextual vectorial flows in motion that interact differentially on forms with flexible internal organizations over time. In other words, the simulated environment is a combination of interconnected force fields whose individual gradients influence the shapes.

As an example, the automotive movement on the highway
41 influenced the north façade of the *H2 House* in Vienna. During animation, a car motion swept several flexible surfaces of the façade and made the interior of the building read as a sequence. Other applied force fields mentioned are generally software related abstractions of external conditions such as pedestrian movement and environmental influences such as wind and sun, to name just a few. Therefore, throughout his projects one can observe this systematic consistency of

motion and transformative aggregation so that the resulting formal expressions appear highly supple and pliant.

Upon close inspection, Greg Lynn's design method combines the process of the fusion of external influences and the internal malleability of the prototype with a consistent amount of improvisation and intuition of the dynamic possibilities. The project's formal expression is at certain stages of the process directed through a critical filter for adaptive provisional prototypes.

Lynn's major interest is in structures known as "blobs" or "meta-balls" from the diverse field of isomorphic polysurfaces. They are monad like primitives with internal forces of attraction and gravitational mass, which are capable of inflecting other objects and join them to aggregates that behave as a singular. The initial programmatic massing, or bubble diagram, in the Korean Church in New York was 42-43 according to this strategy represented through multiple nodes. Their individual spheres of influence then grow into a single "balanced" volume to reach a state of equilibrium. Interactively, these polysurfaces reshape their formation and shape depending on two major factors, the placement within a field of other blobs and their zones of attraction and on the internal force of gravitation assigned to the object. The formal result is called a continuous composite of heterogeneous components that appears as a unit and a multiplicity simultaneously.

ARCHITECTURE OF THE INCOMPLETE: *Jesse Reiser + Nanako Umemoto (RUR Architecture)*

Reiser + Umemoto have the capacity of producing something that can be continuously modifiable and changeable, against a very conventional notion of organization of the building. The repetition of different patterns can be susceptible to infinite variations until it becomes a new soft model. Their work has pursued a rare course of independence and imagination, derived from looking at structural systems capable of engendering complexity through flexibility.

Writing about his own work, Jesse Reiser formulated what he defined as "the practice's task" in the following words:

ARCHITECTURE OF THE INCOMPLETE: REISER+UMEMOTO

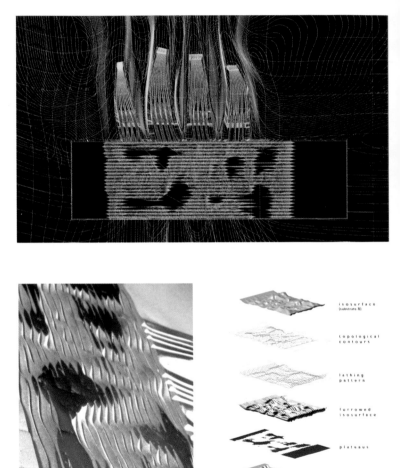

Water Garden (at the Jeff Kipnis residence in suburban Columbus, Ohio, 1997), in collaboration with David Ruy and Jeff Kipnis. Above: wireframe. Middle: left, isometric; right, model closer.

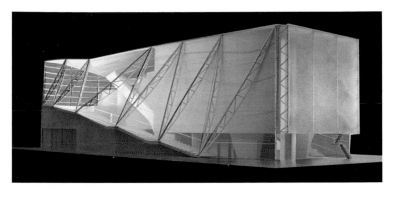

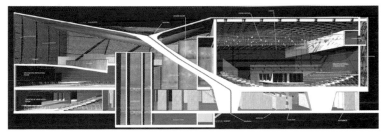

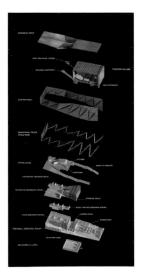

New Tectonics for the Austria Music Theate, Graz, (competition, third prize, 1998). Above: view from the park. Middle: longitudinal section. Below: left, exploded axonometric; right, south elevation.

> [...] chaotic or complex systems. These break with the main binary oppositions that have dominated architecture as a discipline: theory and practice; structure and ornament; global and local; and programme and form. The artificial static of old procedures is broken down and a new fluency and flux inserted in its place. (Reiser, *Loose Fit*)

Reiser + Umemoto are intrigued by the implementation of scientific arguments in architectural language as it appears in the Cardiff Bay Opera House and the Kansay Library competition-projects. Here they approach a tactical use of geodetics, precisely because, as a system, it is capable of adapting to complex spatial transformations, involving the reassessment of Modernism's homogeneous and totalizing architectural languages. Geodetics acts as a structural tissue or flesh that has the capability of adapting to the space developed by it, providing continuous surface effects and enabling relations between the inside and the outside. The smooth movement into the building, through it and within it, defines the building itself and generates programmatic interweavings.

Their focus is shifted from the fixed and static norms of classical geometry to topology, to dynamical, time-based systems: a new horizon of possibilities; a new language of waves; a disquieting, universal structure emerges. The adoption of dynamic diagrams, which have no essential origin and can be incarnated in multiple materials, scales and regimes, find its place. This is not a substrata that one tries to match in a very conventional way, but a continuously changing and workable field. Computer and other forms of modeling are important but the necessary issue is the extension of how one understands the computational behavior of link-systems.

A physical three-dimensional model is a three-dimensional map of digital force-diagrams, generated in a back and forth dance between real and computer models as a way of motivating the formal changes. Theirs is maybe a more interactive version of Gehry's methodology, who used to scan complex manual study-models with the intent of producing computerized drawings having spatial and structural value.

Topological geometry (see "Glossary") develops potentials to engage flows in living and non-living systems. Spatial models as the notions of inside-outside, figure-ground, center-periphery, are reformulated as a complexification. Contingency factors such as site, scale, program, structure and others become mixed with mathematical constructs. The development of topological and complex surfaces becomes, for the last five years of the Reiser + Umemoto practice, the work of animation and computer generation, a device inseparable from the design process itself.

As Andrew Benjamin comments, the problem of formalism is emerging in their work, in which formal innovation is indifferent to function. Innovation on the level of design may leave function unaddressed. Function will be introduced to an already formally construed subject.

There is an ontological distinction between stasis and becoming. The choice between one of them marks out different ways of construing the object-building, different types of architectural practice. Reiser + Umemoto produce new, dynamic, incomplete organizations with temporal implications (what Benjamin calls an "inscription of the future within the present"). Focusing on time-based systems, in the project for a water garden at Jeff Kipnis residence, they had the 48 chance to redefine static models of nature, now modifiable matrices of material becoming, and local transformations as warps, dimples and folds. Within architecture and time, space is either yet to be formed or formed as indeterminate. "The incomplete can only be thought of in relation to the way repetition works within the production of architecture."

In the concept of the project for the Yokohama Port Terminal 44 the differing sense of the incomplete becomes operative. Disruption in terms of perturbation and transformation is applied to an initial structural model. The reiteration, generating difference, of the three-hinged arch "allows for mutations that overcome the idea of linear development, and creates additional spaces and thus sites within the overall structure which are, of course, envisaged as already being part of the structure" (Benjamin 98). The space to come is the space that is already there: the future is already within the present.

52

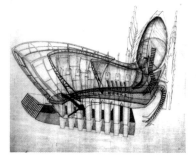

Nonchi Wang (Amphibian Arc), A Monument To Copernicus, *Krakow Planetarium, Poland (competition, first prize, 1993). Above: photo collage of the Monument with the Wszystkich Swietych Square in the foreground. Middle: building elevation with turn-of-the-century municipal building in the background. Below: perspective rendering showing layers of interior spaces and the overlap of exterior shells.*

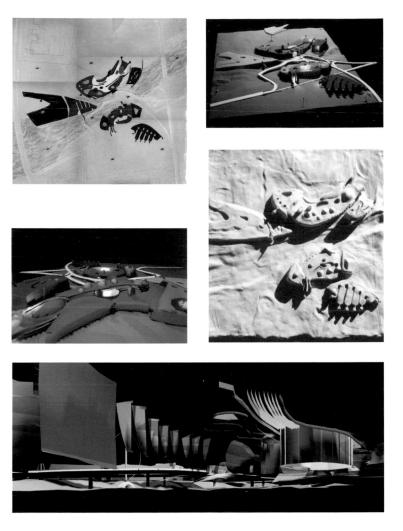

The Service Area of the Logistic Activity Zone (ZAL) of the Port of Barcelona, Spain (competition entry, 1996). Above: left, oil pastel; right, lifted road system weaving through buildings over the riverbed to connect the outside with the ZAL. Middle: right, clay model; left, overall view with the Service Building for personnel and the businesses in the foreground. Below: lifted road system on the riverbed seen through the Service Building.

54

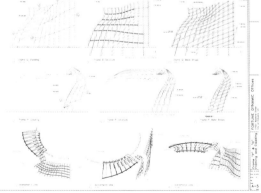

Office Entry for the Fortune Dynamic Company, City of Industry, California (commissioned, March 1998). Above: entrance canopy and freestanding brise-soleil. Below, elevation-details: curvilinear entrance canopy and freestanding brise-soleil, against the existing glass cylinder curtain wall.

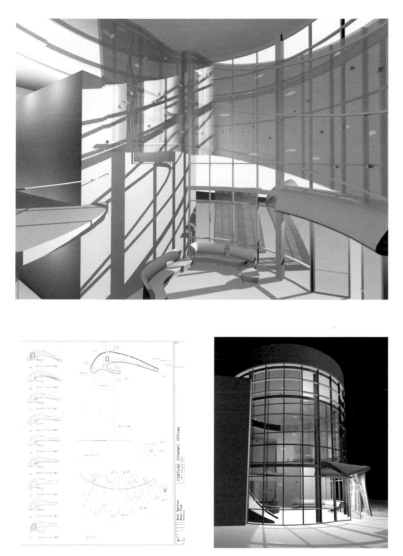

Above: interior perspective, looking from 2nd floor balcony toward outside through the hung brise-soleil. Below: left, elevation-details; right, night-time view of canopy and brise-soleil, and the building lobby.

INTERRUPTED PROJECTIONS: NEIL M. DENARI ARCHITECTS

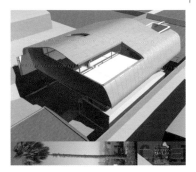

Massey Residence (Schnitt-Haus, 1994). Above: left, aereal view; right: rear elevation detail. Middle: left, section; right, structural X-Ray. Below: night view.

The space for Gallery MA was developed from the Homolosine Interrupted Projection Mapping system. The origin of the word map comes from "sheet", merely a surface to record territories on. The Homolosine Projection depicts the world in a series of sheared ellipses, thus the green surface inside Gallery MA is an "interrupted projection". On the third floor a court-yard equal to the size and proportion of the interior space exists, separated by a membrane of glass. The surface bends and loops to form a three dimensionally smooth yet complex geometry capable of merging with the graphically logo-ized world of visual codes and conventional signs. This is the "worldsheet".

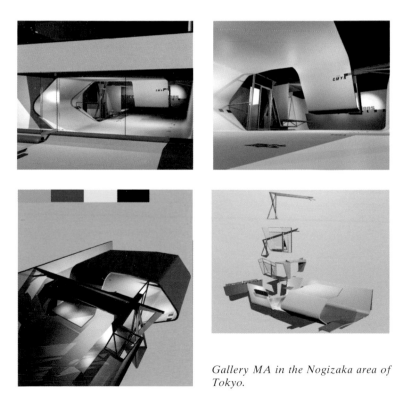

Gallery MA in the Nogizaka area of Tokyo.

Construction: *Summer 1996.* **Production**: *Masaaki Oka;* **Associate Architect**:

58

LIQUID ARCHITECTURE: *Nonchi Wang (Amphibian Arc)*
Amphibian Arc, founded by Hwafong Nonchi Wang in 1992, believes the boundary of architecture expands along with the expanding boundaries of human consciousness.

Since mid-1993, he has been focusing on the idea of Liquid Architecture, (which was coined by Nonchi Wang in 1993 independently from Marcos Novak) an architectural response to the human consciousness that is ever-shifting towards the digital domain in the computer age. Understanding architecture's evolution in the context and on the temporal scale of human evolution, however, defines amphibian Arc's ultimate concern for human habitation.

Nonchi Wang draws inspirations largely from scientific disciplines, such as mathematics, chaos, astrophysics and biology. Metaphors of biological or amphibian origin occur continuously throughout his work. It is a conceptual, rather than critical, design that starts to explore possible ways of conceiving rational buildings which are defined not by formal simplicity but by material complexity.

The spaces he creates are altered, transformed by an alien and antithetic curvilinearity (see "Glossary", *Curved Space*).

By rejecting Euclidean geometries (see "Glossary"), which can not deal with the complexities of nature, Wang used a concept related to Chaos Theory which attempts to unravel the non-linear order and appearance of natural phenomena. Chaos sparks new potentialities of redefining "rationalism" in architecture.

52 In the project site, near two Gothic cathedrals in Krakow, by supporting the structure with a hybrid flying buttresses, he cites Viollet Le Duc rather than the "irrationalism of deconstructionism". Wang is aware of the current trend that endows greater autonomy to computers in form generation. The risk is evident when such exercises and attempts are essentially confined and recognizably shaped by the parameters of the package and software the designer uses.

54-55 As demonstrated in the "Fortune Dynamic Warehouse" project, Wang's digital work is related both to his conceptual and constructed architecture. A precise 3-D computer model is constructed for daylight study as well as for later production of working drawing. The shape of the *brise-soleil* is determined by the sun's path throughout the four seasons reproduced by the computer.

The 3-D model also allows for accurate 2-D graphic representation of structures of irregular geometry for construction and fabrication. (Fortune explanatory text.)

Amphibian Arc has engaged in various types of architectural projects in both public and private realms. It is a matter of daily struggle with budget and program while trying at the same time to import abstractions into real projects.

4.2 In-formation Architecture

INTERRUPTED PROJECTIONS: *Neil M. Denari (Neil M. Denari* 56-57 *Architects)*

The coded systems of the signification strategies in contemporary consumer culture are Denari's major focus of interest, since they have an appropriate response in architecture.

He argues that it is no longer the use value or functional characteristic of the object that directs consumer appetite and the related product marketing. The object may lose its subject or meaning, and because of this then cease to fascinate, since there is no subject within desire. Instead, it is the seductive symbol or sign form of corporate identity that evokes consumer desire and represents the object with an image; its logo.

Our graphic based culture of logos is capable of an endless replication of images through an archive of a rehearsable world image bank. Currently the ubiquity of digital technology yields an overcoding with a second layer of emanating mass media symbols and signifiers. An accumulation of all coded systems worldwide conceptually then replaces the geographic world sphere with a flattened image of new social and economical global alliances.

Thus the concept of real space is reduced to a flat plane of codes; the worldsheet mapped with graphic signifiers. Out of this compressed logo-ized fabric emerges the bent envelope of architectural space as a fully interactive apparatus. The

MEDIATED LIFE. ARCHITECTURE OF TELEMATICS: DILLER + SCOFIDIO

Diller + Scofidio refer to liveness as the mechanism of interactivity that originated in broadcasting, where electronic news is the instantaneous relay of the world. In Jump Cuts, outside a layer of liquid cristal glass appears again

Ventilator, *permanent installation, proposal commissioned by the Museum of Contemporary Art, Chicago 1994*

facing a row of video projectors inside. When the glass is in translucent mode, the direct view between lobby and street is cut off and its video surrogate replaces it. The project allows the viewer to interpret the implications of transparency himself. In Cold War *a video projection screen on ice is used to "thwart the expectations of this audience perched to witness a sporting event". Incorporating movie trailers in* Jump Cuts *or hockey highlights in* Cold War *"means to break down the autonomy of public art from the complex cultural issues of site specificity".*

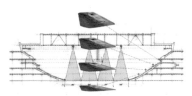

Jump Cuts, *permanent installation at United Artists Cineplex Theater, San Jose, California 1995.* Cold War, *permanent installation in Broward Civic Arena, home of Panthers National Ice Hockey League, Sunrise, Florida, 1997.*

instrumentality of this architecture is therefore a coded layering of elements, such as function, text, shape, material and sign form, that together form a dynamic environment.
Architecture he explains, is an extrapolation machine that excerpts its constituent components from this coded cultural landscape.

> In a world where the currency of the new/now is often valued more than that of tradition, stability, and legibility, what can Architecture, perhaps the heaviest of all disciplines, do to contend with the fluid currencies of money, politics, aesthetics, technoscience, speed, and above all, the world, imagebank which saturates our short-term memory?
>
> THE ANSWER: Make architecture become a currency itself, one capable of changing states fast and with great precision: from *space* to surface to graphic to light and back again. This is not merely another version of the dissipation of building in the face of the contemporary electronic environment. It is a *merger* between the most repetitive and influential sign systems (logos, icons, directives, aphorisms) and the spatial and symbolic potential of Architecture.
>
> My proposition is to design an architecture that responds to the overcoded landscape of signs by investing it with a graphical nature intent on infiltrating the mind, the city, and the eye. As space can be configured around the human body, it can also shape itself around the contours of other value systems like use, exchange, and symbol, those systems that control our cultural/consumerist actions. The scheme for Gallery MA is an overcoded diagram of this concept. (N. Denari, *Interrupted Projection*, explanatory text).

60-61 MEDIATED LIFE. ARCHITECTURE OF TELEMATICS: *Elizabeth Diller and Ricardo Scofidio (Diller + Scofidio)*
They are counted among the most innovative, critical yet affirmative practitioners for their cross-disciplinary approach that explores the junctures of architecture and the visual and performing arts.
Diller + Scofidio use computer and telematics as architectural apparatuses. They also consider films and movie-cameras as important in disseminating information.
Their project-installations have to do with technology, media

and the concept of "the public". Using media and new visual techniques to simulate the real experience of an action, D + S point out that the interaction between recorded images and real-time experience changes our ways of observing social events and daily relationships.

One recent area of their investigations has focused on "liveness" that appeals to both the directions of technophilic and technophobic, as they explain in the following text:

> Proliferating discourses on new media technologies follow two growing tendencies; the technophilic and the technophobic. The technophile's blind love for and assurance in technological progress overrides any concern for the political and economic conditions out of which it is produced. This a-critical embrace of the electronic age, much like the early zealotry of the machine age, stems from a conviction in a radical discontinuity with existing social, political and cultural structures. And like the early years of modernism, the air is thick with the rhetoric of the "new" and the newly obsolete. Technophobes on the other hand, revel in the rhetoric of "loss." The steady incursion of media technologies is blamed for a progressive dismantling of cultural values. Technology is thus posed in moral opposition to home, family and religion. While our work utilizes new technologies, it targets the reductive discourses surrounding them. While the technophilic narratives of progress and the technophobic narratives of decline are at ideological odds with one another, their oppositional framework at times and unexpectedly reveal flip sides of the same desires. One of the biases shared by the techno-extremes is an attraction to "liveness." "Live" is a broadcast term which means simply, now, at this very moment. Liveness holds with it the titillation of the uncut, the uncensored, and the not fully controlled. Liveness turns the passive viewer receiving messages into an eyewitness. For the technophobes who believe that media mediates reality, "liveness" in broadcast may be the last stronghold of auratic or real experience-seeing and/or hearing the event at the precise moment of its occurrence. So long as time is undistorted, immediacy is not entirely surrendered to distance. For technophiles, liveness is the index of technology's ability to simulate the real. Real-time is key. Lag time, delay, search time, download time, response time, feedback time are unwelcome mediations of live-

TRANSFORMAL ARCHITECTURE: WINKA DUBBELDAM (ARCHI-TECTONICS)

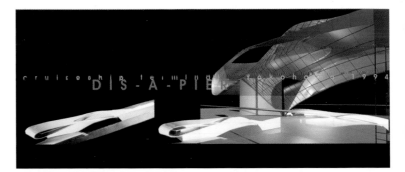

Yokohama Cruise-Ship Terminal, Japan (competition, 1994). Above: perspective view. Below: animation strips.

Millbrook House, State of New York, 1997.

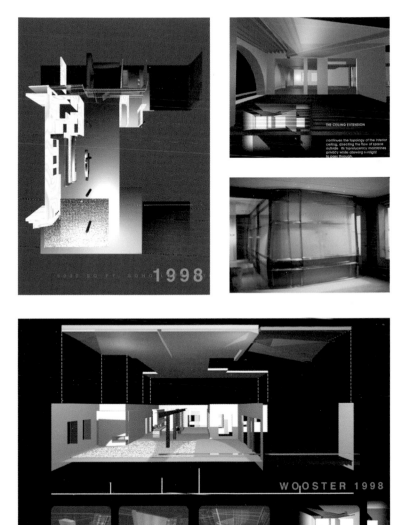

Wooster Loft, New York (completion August 1998). Above: terrace extension. Below: interior wall detail.

ness. Real-time is the speed of computational performance, the ability of the computer to respond to the immediacy of an interaction without temporal mediation. Un-mediated means im-mediate. But, whether motivated by the desire to preserve the real or to fabricate it, liveness is synonymous with the real, and the real is an object of uncritical desire for both techno-extremes. Our present work addresses spatial and temporal "liveness" to "tease" the distinctions between "live" and "mediated" experiences and to collapse those distinctions. (Diller+Scofidio)

TRANSFORMAL ARCHITECTURE: *Winka Dubbledam (Architectonics)*

Her architecture is an experimentation field, in which to explore notions of nomadic, surveyed or dynamic space in reference to Gilles Deleuze, Paul Virilio or Michel Serres, in order to strengthen an ideological vacuum in architecture. Through investigations, similar to comparative approaches in science, alternative strategies are developed in her work that lead a re-conceptualizing of space to counter new infrastructures in post-modern society.

Dubbeldam searches for a dynamic architectural system in a smooth fluid space, a space in constant flux, that has overcome the question of form, a trans-formal space. The characteristic of this space is the expression of a weaving process of layers of functions, landscapes of political, social, economic and cultural influences. Through the notion of the "rhizome" by Gilles Deleuze, these multiple heterogeneous layers without a fixed end or beginning lead her to three typologies of textures, the matrix of a trans-formal Architecture. It is a space of movement, dynamic and temporal, as shown in her 64 focus on arrival and departure in the Yokohama project.

The fluidity of time and space, the experience of temporal delay, the unwinding and interruption of time, is illustrated as a stretching and compression of space and eventually of material and texture.

Space adopts in this project the "behavioral" qualities and the instrumental manifestation of time. The topological model of two twisted rubber bands serves as an ideal metaphor for the space-time relation of the terminal characteristics and investigates the field condition of "urban textures".

The computer is for Dubbeldam a sculpting tool and a conceptual inspiration at the same time. However, it is not only an instrument for the investigation of spatial complexities, but in the era of electronic communication space "a constructive ingredient of the environment". Monitors in the steel wall, a second layered wall behind the exterior landmarks facade of the Christine Rose mixed media art gallery, 28 show the exhibit and its visitors to anyone passing-by on the street. It reverses the perception of viewing to being viewed, and "transforms the dividing wall into an information zone".

It is also an example of a smart membrane, a mediated screen, that replaces a wall function of protection into "the electronic surveillance zone of cameras and sensors", thus referring to Dubbeldam's second typology of Architectural Textures. Layers of various surfaces refer to materials such as glass and steel and transform walls, floors and windows.

In the Soho Loft, translucent, suspended and pivoting planes 65 are introduced as connective membranes to interlock volumes. Through the method of slicing planes, one is able to occupy several programmatic zones simultaneously. Here interwoven flows of communication and continuous space create fields of occupation. One can trace similarities to the dynamic connection of permeable zones that transform the exchange of the Millbrook House with its exterior into a set 64 of spatial events.

Referring to nomadic qualities, but still forming a node in the global information network, Dubbeldam talks about a constant flow of new media, the Virtual Textures. Again planes, glass walls, voids and partly enclosed spaces render the house porous and "mediate space and vision".

Throughout her projects, the representation of material and immaterial flows, a trans-formal mixture of the real and the informational space, reconstructs an artificial fluid urban milieu.

TRANSARCHITECTURES - LIQUID ARCHITECTURE: MARCOS NOVAK

This page and facing page: Paracube *project.*

TRANSARCHITECTURES -LIQUID ARCHITECTURE: *Marcos Novak*

In the creation of a navigable-electronic non-place that can be experienced as a fully dimensional space, architecture is the "interface to the imagination". Virtual reality is the enabling technology and cyberspace is the content. Combined they are the worlds of cyberspace, the exterior of virtual reality and the possible worlds of our invention. Here the physics are invented, the singular can be replaced by the multiple, the solid by the fragmented, the closed by the open.

Now that the cinematic image has become habitable and interactive, any boundary has been crossed irrevocably, and thousands of virtual communities are forming on networks everywhere. For Novak, Net-nations may emerge spatially, temporally and ideologically unrestricted, that have rapidly fluctuating populations and topologies.

Cyberspaces as whole and networked virtual environments in particular, allow us to construct "spaces for human inhabitation" in a completely new kind of electronic non-local, public realm and to think in terms of genetic engines of artificial life.

> When bricks become pixels, the tectonics of architecture becomes informational. City planning becomes data structure design, construction costs become computational costs, and accessibility becomes Transmissibility.

A cyberspace architecture would change interactively as a function of duration, use, and external influence. Nonlinear, its different states would yield efficient transmission via a coded notation of the multiple and mediate endlessness.

Thus the discipline of architecture is being redefined by replacing all constants with variables, such as the total mutability of form, which leads to the idea of *Liquid Architecture*. This involves again the re-problematization of time as an active element of architecture.

"Liquid architecture makes liquid cities that change at the timely shift of a value, where visitors with different backgrounds see different landmarks".

ARCHITECTURE OF IMAGE: HANI RASHID + LISE ANNE COUTURE
(ASYMPTOTE ARCHITECTURE)

Here galleries, libraries, theaters, cinemas, parks, and plazas all intersect the fluid and transient space of the city. The Steel Cloud is architecture for the post-information age, devoid of perspective, depth, frames, or enclosure; it is a prop for a place where hallucination and fiction temper vivid reality.

Los Angeles West Coast Gateway, The Steel Cloud, *1989.*

Architecture of image: Hani Rashid + Lise Anne Couture (Asymptote Architecture)

Above: Hyperfine Splitting. *Middle and below:* Optigraph 4 – 001, Optigraph 4 – 003.

Aarhus Univers Theaters, Denmark, 1996

Past the influence of modernity and on the way to the next paradigm of virtuality, we are moving in a transversal link, which Novak termed Transmodernity.

Transformative exponential change and the proliferation of a transversal weaving and warping of hypersurfaces constitute the notion of *Transarchitectures* (see "Glossary").

The resulting conditions are transmutations into unpredictable conceptual spaces, explorations that reveal tectonic materials whose potencies and valences cannot immediately be comprehended.

> The alternative to the omnivorousness is to produce an endless proliferation of alien variety, pushing towards a transevolutionary transmutation.

His work is a research into virtual tectonics, where he constructs mathematical algorithmic models and generative procedures that are constrained by numerous variables, initially unrelated to any pragmatic concerns. Each variable or process is a "slot" into which an external influence can be mapped. Once the model is constructed, an interactive evolutionary process locates a set of values that fit into the different slots and instantiates a design.

These values can be derived from particulars of the real world, from data and processes of the virtual world or from numerous techniques of capturing the real and casting it into the virtual. If time is a feature of the model, the form becomes animate, the architecture-liquid. A notion of abstract continuity is implied and introduces the invariant algorithm, the new variable topology.

While the variations of parameters that implement the algorithm may be continuous, the product of the algorithm may be discontinuous and fractured into a cloud of particles.

> I compute or find a field of forces or data, scan it for isosurfaces, extrude the isosurfaces into a hyperspace of higher dimension, transform the new higher dimensional hyperobjects in the hyperspace, project the object in a space of fewer dimensions – a *hypersurface* of the

hyperspace – [see "Glossary", *Hypersurface, Hyperspace*] and then, finally, warp the spatial matrix itself into a new curvature of space. (*Transtexts*).

The design does not end with form: it is the hypersurface of the interface that animates the design.

ARCHITECTURE OF IMAGE: *Hani Rashid and Lise-Anne Couture (Asymptote Architecture)*
From their *Steel Cloud* project for LA in 1989 through the 71 Yokohama Bay project in 1996, each form has emerged from the interpretation and reading of many layers of contextual, phenomenal and cultural strata that surround the site, program and meaning of the building they were designing. Lately, they are interested in form generation through the use of computers, however they think that the computer outputs are insignificant without the incorporation of the above mentioned preoccupations.

Many of Asymptote's projects "inhabit" the space of virtual reality, taking meaninglessness, indeterminacy and unreasonableness of form as the conditions of their research. The computer is used to be transgressive, allowing the production of new types of "sketches" in the realm of the filmic, the sonic, and the textual.

The investigation of the phenomenal terrain includes subjects and objects, from the material to the transcendental, tending however toward the immaterial. When working in virtual reality, architecture is the result of many other dynamics such as movement, sound, interactivity, luminosity and narrative.

Asymptote's work is involved in the space between the conceptual and the implementable and in this way is critical and discursive, orientated towards other territories and external interests. For the most part their zones of research involve film, media, visual arts, and visual culture. The answer to noise, distraction, movement, flows, transpacific flight, blur, the Internet, fluxes, plastics, PhotoShop, VRML, speed (data) transience and liquidity, comes with an architecture that is one of overlap, opposition, simultaneity, where hierarchy is

ARCHITECTURE OF IMAGE: HANI RASHID + LISE ANNE COUTURE
(ASYMPTOTE ARCHITECTURE)

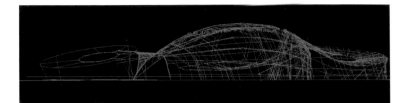

Kyoto Multimedia facilities, 1995. Kyoto Multimedia Research Park and Edutainment and Technology Museums, Japan, second phase, completion by the end of 2000.

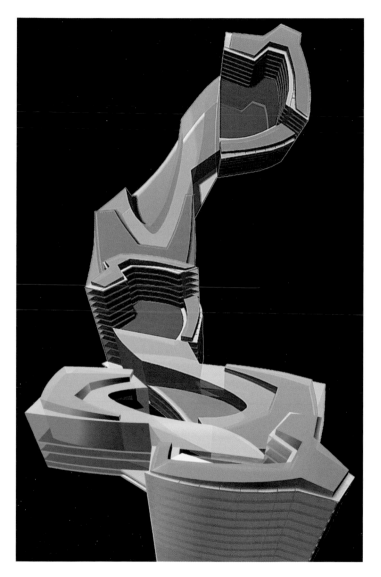

Kyoto Multimedia Facilities, *1995. Kyoto Multimedia Research Park and Edu-tainment and Technology Museums, Japan.*

78

undetermined, neither site nor object dominate. Asymptote's projects are provocative and complex, versus an open ended that oscillates between the static and the dynamic, the fixed and the indeterminate, the tactile and the intangible. It is the space of uncontrolled events, a field of possibilities.

72 They are architects of image, of apparatuses without monumentality or fixity. The experimental studies defined as "Optigraphs" analyze processes associated with optic experiences, calling into question our timeworn visual practices.

> The *Optigraphs* began as 'surveillances' of found images extracted from newspapers, magazines, travel brochures, technical manuals, entertainment guides, television, advertising, and any other medium offering evidence of the cult of the image. This processing, recording, and play back, combined with phenomenological vectors such as noise, distraction, anonymity, delirium, and hallucination, yielded architectures that peered precariously beneath the last vestiges of modernity, revealing concealed territories of enigma, strangeness and delusion. (Rashid, *Monograph* 95).

72 The methods of the *Optigraphs* and the *Hyperfine Splitting* investigate, through sophisticated computer software, a non-objective and non-finite architecture.
They are dealing with the dispersion or dissolution of the object-building.

> *Hyperfine Splitting* addresses the impact of the computer on all aspects of human activity. In this series we used digital photography, scanning, video animation, drawing and modeling to capture architectural moments in an otherwise continuous, fluid action of making space [...] A space emerges, made only of light. (Rashid, *Monograph* 95).

Asymptote proposes a reconfiguration of architecture through a radical mutation of its relation to space as an abstract referent, the one-dimensional space of geometry. Measure based on Cartesian geometry is replaced by a multiplicity of infinitesimal dimensions at once spatial and qualitative. Geometry in and of itself is not an issue. Each geometric principal and approach offers fascinating and provocative possibilities for architecture.

The question is not so much which is an appropriate one to adopt or subscribe to, but rather what does each reveal and imply about the spatiality we are creating. The alliance of geometry with structure and economy and the parallel condition of geometry are mechanisms for perception and comprehension.

Asymptote considers every site of intervention a set of givens, a collection of information the architect must organize and rewrite in his work, in a state of perpetual transformation. There is no difference between the programmatic and functional issues of the architectural and conceptual project. Program, function, structure and economy are all equally interesting territories on which to develop a conceptual approach that concerns musicality, flux, distortion and others. Rashid and Couture are working both within and without the tradition of architecture, in a "precise misalignment" with history, with expected emotions, with conventional typologies.

"You pursue the program with all the rigor and responsibility of the architect, but at the same time you look for those nuances of contradiction" (Rashid, *Monograph* 95).

FROM COMPLEXITY TO THE BANAL. ARCHITECTURE OF THE 80-82
EVERYDAY: *Thomas Leeser (Leeser Architecture)*
Leeser's present position has reached a turning point. It is his conviction that the word "formal" is heavily loaded with negative connotations. Since everything does have some form, even writing, the question is more what value do you assign to it. Form conveys meaning in architecture. It is an integral part of its language that can be spoken conservatively or critically.

The problem arrives when this criticality becomes absorbed in a conservative discourse. It becomes an agent of diffusion with the effect of debasing the once critical strategy by transmutating it into a mere style. Unfortunately, he insists, this is what is happening right now. Leeser's work has always aimed at questioning the *status quo* by challenging the convention of the

FROM COMPLEXITY TO THE BANAL. ARCHITECTURE OF THE EVERYDAY: THOMAS LEESER (LEESER ARCHITECTURE)

Max-Planck Research Institute, Munich, Germany (National Building Design Competition, 1993). Facing page: Wallraf-Richartz Museum, Cologne, Germany (international competition, 1996).

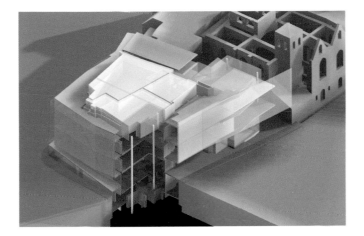

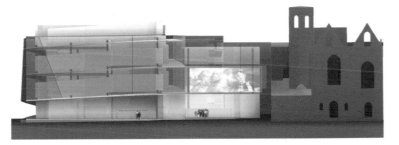

FROM COMPLEXITY TO THE BANAL: ARCHITECTURE OF THE EVERYDAY
THOMAS LEESER (LEESER ARCHITECTURE)

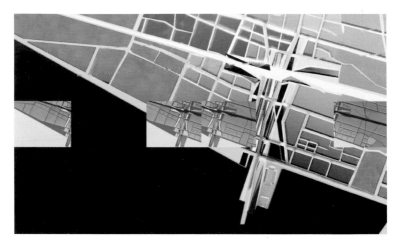

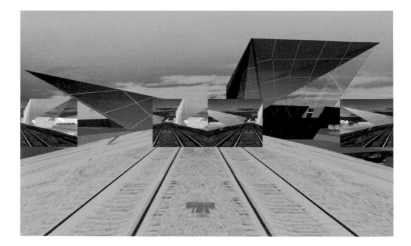

Gamagory City, Aichi Prefecture, Japan (Urban Design Proposal, 1994).

language of architecture. When functional and conventional programmatic arguments were the basis for what people understood as the primary means of the production of architecture, it was important to develop alternative strategies.

The integration and inclusion of "other disciplines" is still essential in expressing complex cultural phenomena. However, the work Leeser did in the eighties, which included all sorts of ideas, particularly those from science, has had its day. Now that those goals have been achieved at least within the academic communities to such a degree that it has become the new *status quo*, it is crucial for Leeser to rethink what it means to be radical.

Deconstruction has become the predominant language of architecture at schools across the US and abroad. There is little radicality left in it. As he tried to outline, the conformist and reactionary have begun to assimilate this language depriving it of its once potent meaning. That is why his recent work has shifted towards a literal consideration of issues of function and program, making them the very basis for what is called conceptualized architecture.

Most of his early work could be understood as "folded", even though he does not think that a categorization is necessarily helpful in understanding the intent of it. The issue of complex geometry was a crucial field of exploration in opening up the narrow definition of architecture. But for him it has suddenly lost a lot of its effectiveness and urgency. Complex geometry to a large extent has become a style, effectively voiding it of its original intention.

The *Twin House* is the only project where he used a diagram for its implicit relevance to the issues he was interested in exploring at the time.

Another of Leeser's crucial questions is: "What does this or any other diagram signify, and what is its relevance?" Only then can one decide if the diagram carries any potential for the understanding of new spatial and cultural possibilities. If it does, it may be a possible strategy for developing an architectural position.

It unfortunately becomes a common assumption or maybe

implication that merely using the computer means resisting normalization. Probably precisely for the reason that the use of computers almost automatically assumes the representation of cutting edge, radical work, which he absolutely does not subscribe to, he has turned his interest to issues of the Normal and the Banal. It is the everyday that has become the largest resistor to any change.

Further Reading

1. THE NEW SCENE

1.1 Rethinking Traditional Architectural Assumptions
Van Berkel and Bos, "Real space in quick times pavilion", in *Hypersurface Architecture, A.D. Profile*, no. 133, 1998.

1.2 From CAADesign to CAADesigners
Christopher Alexander, "The Question of Computers in Design", in *Landscape*, Autumn 1967; John Frazer, "An Evolutionary Architecture", Themes VII, in *AA*, London 1995.

1.3 Crossing Disciplines
The 2nd International Conference on Evolvable Systems, in ETH Lausanne, combined the power of computer-designers, biologists, physicists and engineers to develop the next generation of computer hardware, adapting solutions of nature to technical problems. T. Luethi, C. Speicher, F. Wuersten, "Computer-designer auf den Spuren Darwins", in *Neue Zuercher Zeitung*, 30-09-1998. See also J. Frazer, *Datastructures for rule-based and genetic design*, in *Visual Computing-Integrating Computer Graphics with Computer Vision*, Springer Verlag, Heidelberg 1992.

1.4 Fluid, Seamless Integration
Sanford Kwinter, *Soft Systems*, Brian Boigon, Culture Lab 1, Princeton Architectural Press, New York 1995.

2. THE YOUNG AMERICAN ARCHITECTS

2.1 Sons without Fathers
Until recently conventional computer graphics was essentially Euclidean, i.e. rigid, polygonal and flat. The consequence was that the quality of human forms such as subtly reactive soft tissues, or muscle-bone dynamics of motion were hard to model. Perrella Stephen, Computer Imaging, Folding in Architecture, *A.D. Profile*, no. 102, 1993. "Recombinant architecture will happen [...] at the level of particles of building types, [...] all morphed into strange new evanescent forms [...]". Marcos Novak, *TransUrban Optimism after the Maul of America*, a critical text on William J. Mitchell, *City of Bits*, MIT-Press, Cambridge 1995 (http://www.ctheory. com). Morphing related to the act of becoming in Gilles Deleuze, Félix Guattari, *A Thousand Plateaus: Capitalism and Schizophrenia*, Minnesota Press, Minneapolis 1987. On the relationship of fathers/sons: Instead of Eisenman's dislocative forms, questioning the metaphysic of architecture, destabilizing the interiority of functional humanism that dominated modernism and still persists today, Lynn wants to move architecture from this interiority to its exteriority, from static form to new "animate form" which interacts with the dynamics of its urban context. More about this formal newness of the contemporary American architects in Michael Speaks: "It's out there. The formal limits of the American Avant-Garde", in *A.D. Profile*, no. 133. On Peter Eisenman from the early projects to the current works see, among many others: Peter Eisenman, Maria-Rita Perbellini, Christian Pongratz, "The Possibility of Redefinition", in *Korean Architects*, no. 156, 1997. The citation

comes from a conversation between Peter Eisenman and Alan Balfour reported in *AA Files 25*.

2.2 Tools and Effects

The integration of design-engineering- manufacturing (CAD/CAE/CAM) allows for rapid prototyping and flexible production. Anthony Webster, *Automation and Artisanry in Architecture*, lecture at Columbia University, Nov. 1996.

2.3 Influences without Geography

With a collection of texts and projects, Stan Allen helps to clarify architecture's role in the new city. Architects have answered in two ways: with a secure return to the certainties of architecture's traditional forms and conventional boundaries; or affiliating architecture with film and video, science, new technology and virtual realities. More fundamental shifts are required. "Science, ideology and technique must be reread as already architectural". Stan Allen, *Its exercise, under certain conditions*, Columbia Documents of Architecture and Theory, Vol. III, New York 1993. Virginia Wolf, as cited from Stan Allen: "To be fully part of the crowd and at the same time completely outside it, removed from it: to be on the edge, to take a walk like Virginia Woolf (never again will I say: 'I am this, I am that'). *Mrs. Dalloway* as cited in G. Deleuze, F. Guattari, *A Thousand Plateaus* cit., p. 29.

2.4 The Breeding Ground

Information on program of studies, faculty members, services of American schools of architecture, colleges, universities is easily accessible on the web: http://www.cranbrook.edu; http://arch.columbia.edu; http://www.cooper.edu; http://www.gsd.harvard.edu; http://www.IIT.edu; http://alberti.mit.edu; http://www.princeton.edu; http://www.rice.edu; http://www.sciarc.edu; http://www.ucla.edu.

3. PREMEDITATION

3.1 An "Intermedial" Architecture

Paul Virilio elaborated (in *Architecture Principe*, issue 1) on the function of the oblique (third spatial dimension) as the architectonic implementation of topology, a way of pleating the ground. "Euclidean geometry has built architecture from early history until modernity. Tomorrow we will build with topology." Enrique Limon, *Paul Virilio and the Oblique*, in *Sites & Stations, Provisional Utopias*, Lusitania Press, New York 1995. *Landform Architecture*, generally display concerns for organic metaphors, such as geological formations or fractal languages. It appears as artificial landscape. Charles Jencks, "Nonlinear Architecture", in *New Science = New Architecture*, A.D. Profile, no. 129, 1997. Id., *The architecture of the jumping universe*, Academy Editions, London 1995. Peter Weibel, "Intelligent Ambients-Environments of Artificial Intelligence, Intelligent Environment", in *Ars Electronica*, no. 94. Roy Ascot, *Apparitional Aesthetics*, Prix Ars Electronica 95, International Compendium of the Computer Arts, ORF. On philosophy and its impact on architecture at different moments: Mark Wigley, *The Architecture of Deconstruction, Derrida's Haunt*, MIT Press, Cambridge 1993; Gilles Deleuze, Félix Guattari, *Anti-Oedipus. Capitalism and Schizophrenia*, University of Minnesota Press, Minneapolis 1987; Bernard Tschumi, *Architecture and Disjunction*, The MIT

Press, Cambridge and London 1984. From Kipnis: the term "Deformation" groups projects with topologies that cannot be reduced into simple planar constituents or referred to the abstraction of modernist formalism. "Information" groups projects that incorporate disparate programmatic and formal components in a neutral modernist monolith. Residual spaces are activated with visual layering, programmatic innovation, technological events and effects. Jeffrey Kipnis, "Towards a New Architecture", in *A.D. Profile*, no. 102. On formalism in architecture: Andrew Benjamin, *Opening Resisting Forms* (in *Recent Projects of Reiser + Umemoto*, Academy Editions, London 1998) and "Resisting Ambivalence, The doubling of function in Eisenman's architecture", in *Korean Architects*, no. 156, 1997.

3.2 Topological Surfaces (De-formation)

"Topological smooth form", in Deleuzian terms is a development of form which is referred to as the "continuous variation" (G. Deleuze, F. Guattari, *A Thousand Plateaus* cit., p. 478). S. Kwinter calls a system soft, when it is flexible, adaptable and evolving. It has a complex organization, maintained by a dense network of active information or feedback loops (Kwinter, *Soft Systems*). A form, therefore in any scale follows a curvilinear trajectory only under the impulsion of derivative, compressive or elastic forces, that determine the curve through the mechanical notion of the surrounding bodies or forces on the outside. Gilles Deleuze, *The Fold, Leibniz and the Baroque. The Pleats of Matter*, Minnesota Press, Minneapolis 1993. Brian Massumi defines "virtual reality" as the reality of change: the event. He argues that the virtual is therefore not contained in any actual form assumed by things or its states. It runs in the transitions from one form to another. It has an unformed abstract state of a reality that may evolve in a variety of possibilities. Brian Massumi, "Sensing the Virtual, Building the Insensible", in *A.D. Profile*, no. 133.

3.3 Hypersurfaces

Hypersurfaces reflect an emerging architectural condition that resists any classical definition. They are generated from combined dynamics of mediatised culture. See also Stephen Perrella, "Hypersurface Theory: Architecture >< Culture", in *A.D. Profile*, no. 133. J. Kipnis suggests that any new architecture seeking to contribute to a non-hierarchical, heterogeneous political space, must meet five characteristics: "vastness, blankness, pointing, incongruity and intensive coherence" (J. Kipnis, *Towards a New Architecture* cit.).

4. DIFFERENCES

4.1 De-formation Architecture

MODAL SPACE: *Karl Chu*

According to Leibniz, Chu states, monads are microautomata propelled by metaphysical force. K. Chu, "The Cone of Immanenscendence", Diagram Work, in *ANY 23*, 1998. "Genetic space is the domain of the set of possible worlds generated and mitigated by the machinic *phylum* over time". It derives "from the physical and the machinic sphere of virtuality forming a topology of an hourglass". K. Chu, "Genetic Space, Hourglass of the Demiurge", in *AD Profile*, 1998. Modal constructivism includes diverse notions such as generative systems, self-organizations, nonlinear dynamics, artificial life, complexity, morphogenetic potentials and other theories. K. Chu, "Modal space: The Virtual Anatomy of Hyperstructures", in *Architects in Cyberspace, A.D. Profile,* no. 118, 1995.

ANIMATE FORM: *Greg Lynn*
Similar also to viscous fluids, the pliant mixture offers, with his methodologies, an internal organization that is either flexible or weak enough to be formally dependent on certain external constraints. "Assumed is an abstract material of ideal deformability which can be deformed, with the exception of disruption." G. Lynn, "Architectural Curvilinearity, The Folded, the Pliant and the Supple", in *AD,* no. 102, 1993. Other suggested publications by Lynn: *Projects,* in *Sites and Stations, Provisional Utopias,* Lusitania Press, New York 1995; "Forms of Expression", in *El Croquis,* no. 72, 1995; *Folds, Bodies & Blobs: Collected Essays,* Encore Books by Architects, Brussels 1998; *Animate Form,* Book and Interactive CD-ROM, Princeton Press, New York 1999; *ANY Magazine,* Editorial Board Member, 1992-present.

ARCHITECTURE OF THE INCOMPLETE: *Reiser + Umemoto*
J. Reiser, *Loose Fit,* in Andrew Benjamin, *Reiser + Umemoto, recent projects,* Academy Editions, London 1998. Their description of the Cardiff Bay Opera House project (Wales, competition entry, 1994) contains more information on Geodetics. *Geodesis* (from the Greek), imaginary geographical lines following the curvature of the earth along straight paths. On organic and non organic systems: R+U took the concept of the "machinic phylum" (G. Deleuze, *op. cit.*; see also K. Chu), a set of self-organizing processes in the universe, in which organic and non-inorganic elements suddenly reach a critical point at which they begin to "cooperate" to form a higher level entity (see explanatory text of Water Garden project). A. Benjamin, *Reiser + Umemoto, recent projects* cit. On the question of the new within architecture and the temporal gap between form and function: J. Rajchman, *What is New in Architecture,* in *Philosophical Events: Essay of the '80s,* Columbia Press, New York 1991, p. 62.

LIQUID ARCHITECTURE: *Nonchi Wang*
Copernicus was educated in Krakow between 1491-95 and set in motion the downfall of Ptolemaic astronomy by postulating that the earth revolved around the sun. In his book (*De Revolutionibus Orbium Coelestium*), Copernicus proposed that the Sun, not the Earth, was the center of the universe. Hwafong Nonchi Wang, "A Monument to Copernicus-Krakow Planetarium. Architecture of the Space Machine", in *Korean Architects,* no. 10, 1994

4.2 In-formation Architecture

INTERRUPTED PROJECTIONS: *Neil Denari*
Interrupted Projections, his first book published in 1996 in Tokyo, explores the contemporary landscape of advertising, media saturation and the effects of displacement (digital) technology in our time. Representing the earth on a flat surface (sheet), is most often used for its accuracy in depicting landforms. Unlike the Mercator projection which flattens and distorts the world into a pure Cartesian atlas-like grid, the Homolosine is irregular in its form as it is cut out along various longitudinal meridians. Suggested short list of publications from Neil Denari: "Intransigent Desires", in *ANY Magazine,* no. 10, 1995; *Recent Work,* E.S.P. Publications Co., Ltd., Bangkok 1996; *Gyroscopic Horizons,* Princeton Press, New York, forthcoming Fall 1999.

ARCHITECTURE OF TELEMATICS: *Diller + Scofidio*
For their project's extensive description see on web: *Diller + Scofidio, tech90s, Transcript.* Elizabeth Diller and Ricardo Scofidio published: *Back to the Front: Tourisms of War*, Princeton Architectural Press, New York 1994; *Flesh*, Princeton Architectural Press, New York 1995, second printing 1998.

TRANSFORMAL ARCHITECTURE: *Winka Dubbeldam*
Her work can be found in the monograph: *Winka Dubbeldam Architect*, published by 010 Publishers, Rotterdam 1996. See also: Georgi Stanishev, "Trans Formal Architecture", in *World Architecture*, Oct. 1996; Michael Speaks, "A New views of the observer: Dubbeldam, Diller & Scofidio", in *Space*, Sept. 1995.

TRANSARCHITECTURES - LIQUID ARCHITECTURE: *Marcos Novak*
"Trans" = neither modern nor post-modern. The term "transArchitectures" is intended to break down the polar opposition of physical to virtual and propose in its stead a continuum ranging from physical architecture to architecture energized by technological augmentation to the architecture of cyberspace. Suggested readings by Marcos Novak: "Tierra Trans Form", in *Medien. Kunst. Passagen*, no. 3, 1994; *Computation and Composition*, and *Breaking The Cage* in *Architecture as a Translation of Music*, Pamphlet Architecture 16, Princeton Architectural Press, New York 1994; *Liquid Architectures in Cyberspace*, in *Cyberspace: First Steps*, MIT Press, Cambridge 1991. Novak is the founding editor of *Centrifuge*, a CD ROM and World Wide Web based electronic journal.

ARCHITECTURE OF IMAGE: *Asymptote*
Liberation from representation and from Cartesian geometry allows the creation of forms that are an "utterance without language" and architecture "outside building and traditional notion of place". See "H. Rashid + L.A.Couture, Architects' statement", in *A+U*, no. 283, 1994. *Opti-graph* (from the Greek *optikos*, in other sense, and *graphein*, to write) derives from new representations of the technique of collage through digital technology. Publications by Asymptote: H. Rashid + L.A. Couture, "Architexturing Copenhagen", in *A.D. Profile*, no. 133, pp. 62-65; *Architecture for the Future, Asymptote Architecture*, Pierre Terrail Editions, Paris 1996, pp. 171-173; *Asymptote: Architecture at the Interval. Rashid + Couture*, Rizzoli International, New York 1995, monograph. On their architectural approach: Deborah Fausch, "The opposition of Postmodern Tectonics. At the Asymptote", in *Tectonics Unbound, ANY Magazine*, no. 14, 1996.

ARCHITECTURE OF THE EVERYDAY: *Thomas Leeser*
By T. Leeser: *The Architecture of Navigation, Three installations with students from Columbia University, NY and Melbourne University*, Australia 1999 (forthcoming); *Chora L. Works: A Collaboration between P. Eisenman and J. Derrida*, editors J. Kipnis and Th. Leeser, Monacelli Press, New York - London 1997; (with P. Eisenman and R. Rizzi), *Moving Arrows, Eros and other Errors. An Architecture of Absence*, The Architectural Association, Box 3, AA Publications, London 1986.

Glossary

Cinematic sectioning: Method of controlling the design of large structures. The shape is mostly that of a landform building, where analysis by cutting infinite sections in sequence reveals self-similar slices.

Complexity theory: the theory of an emergent organization, pushed from a position of equilibrium to the limit between order and chaos, to that point of phase transition where it is self-organizing, developing new organizational levels of its parts.

Curved space: Riemannian geometry (a non-Euclidean system based on the postulate that within a plane every pair of lines intersects) led to and made possible the concepts used by Albert Einstein in his General Theory of Relativity. The two studies are indispensable devices in describing mathematically curved space-time (for ex., 4-dimensional space). "The fact that a light beam curves at the presence of a celestial body then, logically, suggests the shortest distance between two points could be a curved line. The only explanation is that the space itself is curved under the gravitational pull of the celestial body" (N. Wang).

Deterministic chaos: the behavioral quality of a system that only appears to be completely random. However, if the system keeps running long enough, the probability of behavior can be predicted within certain limits with a mathematical equation (see Edward Lorenz's strange attractor graph).

Dynamical systems theory: study of processes in nonlinear motion and their behavior.

Epigenetic landscape: a shape that describes the relationship of an evolving form or simpler organs and their differentiation within an environment.

Euclidean geometry: "Holds that space is three dimensional and 'flat'. The Flatness of the 3-D space demands: the shortest distance between two points is a straight line: this omits the possibility of curved space. Circles, squares and triangles are the most representative shapes of Euclidean geometry" (N. Wang).

Fractal geometry: deals with the underlying order of many seemingly chaotic phenomena and with the most complex geometrical orders found in Nature. It describes "the complexity of nature. Two essential properties of fractal geometry are self-similarity and infinite details" (N. Wang).

Hyperspace: "Space, as we know it, is both non-Euclidean or curved and multidimensional, containing more than three spatial dimensions." Physical spaces (empirical rigor) and possible spaces (logical rigor): "In either case we now think of n-dimensional manifolds" (M. Novak).

Hypersurface: "A hypersurface of a hyperspace of (n)-dimensions is a submanifold of ($n-1$) dimensions. Thus the hypersurface of a hyperspace of 4 spatial dimensions is a space of 3 spatial dimension" (M. Novak).

Morphing: smoothly interpolates two different states of formal aggregation into one continuous shape. Its importance is the capability of mutation and transplacement of certain characteristics of one configuration into other unlimited instances. It involves a transformation between objects of completely different shapes, sizes and forms.

Nonlinear systems: systems capable of self-organization, and thus that can spontaneously create order, through often more than one equilibrium state, bifurcation points and transitions from one stable trajectory to another. They are autonomous and certain generic properties may appear despite differentiated systems and contexts.

Neo-darwinism: through random (genetic) mutations the phenotype (or shape) changes in appearance. In certain cases, the successive selection process decides certain changes to be advantageous and one prototype is selected which may lead, in the following process, to an evolutionary change with respect to historical development.

Panopticism: in Foucault's terms of panopticism, concrete architectural form is transformed into abstract machinic instrumentality and technology as an expression of cultural, social, and political relation. These notions see architecture as the catalyst of infrastructural form with unlimited possibilities for transformation and configuration.

Simulation: visual substitute for real artifacts.

Symmetry breaking: the methodology that allows an open, flexible adaptive system to increase its organization.

Stereo-reality: with this term, Paul Virilio defined the stereoscopic effect of the doubling of the real by the virtual.

Topological geometry: a supple geometry capable, because of its flexibility, of reacting to external events and being deformed into a continuous smooth space. These curvilinear forms are shaped by their specific context and environment and are not representations of these external conditions and forces.

Transarchitecture: a multithreaded architecture that weaves together the informational and the material, the virtual and the actual, the possible and the real. Rooted in notions of metamorphosis, the prefix "trans" signifies a condition of change (M. Novak).

Virtuality: Invisible inherent properties and behavior of the components of a system that determine the possibilities of future formal development.

Virtual reality: the term Virtual and its combination with reality in the prevailing mis-conception as simulation (simulated reality) or artificiality, especially in its implementation in digital-architectural design, does not describe its actual implications in the current realm of the computational age. Instead, following an alternative interpretation of Deleuze and Guattari, it is an assumed reality or a mode of reality implicated in the emergence of new potentials. It refers to a certain configuration that has the potentiality for a possible differentiation.

Profiles

Karl S. Chu (Xkavya). Presently teaching at Sci-Arc in Los Angeles, he is originally from Burma and acquired his Master of Architecture degree from the Cranbrook Academy of Art, Michigan. He has been published in numerous international magazines and has lectured and exhibited worldwide. His work and interest are directed towards the metaphysics of architecture and computation. *metaxy@earthlink.net.*

Greg Lynn (Form). Presently teaching at the GSAP of Columbia University in New York and at UCLA in Los Angeles, he graduated from Miami University of Ohio with two degrees (in Philosophy and Environmental Design), and from Princeton University with a Master of Architecture degree. His projects have been widely published and exhibited. He has worked in the architectural offices of P. Eisenman and A. Predock. His office, Form, is presently working in partnership with M. McInturf Architects on the master plan of the Cincinnati Country Day School in Ohio, on the Hydrogen House for the OMV Corporation in Vienna, Austria and also on the Vision Plan for Rutgers University in collaboration with Eisenman Architects in New York. G. Lynn Form, M. McInturf Architects and D. Garofalo Architects collaborated on the design of the Korean Presbyterian Church of New York. *glynn@idt.net; http://www.a-node.net; http://www. basilisk.com.*

Reiser + Umemoto (Rur Architecture). Both teach at the GSAP of Columbia University. J. Reiser studied at Cooper Union in New York and completed his Master of Architecture at the Cranbrook Academy of Art; N. Umemoto graduated from Cooper Union following his studies at the School of Urban Design at the Osaka University of Art. RUR Architecture P.C. since 1986, has been a specialist in large-scale, infrastructural urban developments. Most recently the firm developed proposals for the East River front of Manhattan, as well as being selected as one of the five participants in a competition focusing on the West Side of Manhattan sponsored by the International Foundation for the Canadian Center for Architecture. Their work has been widely published and exhibited in the US, Japan and Europe. *rurarch@inch.com.*

Nonchi Wang (Amphibian Arc). Studied at Tunghai University, Taiwan and the Yale School of Architecture where he earned a master's degree in the Environmental Design program. Since 1994, he has had his own practice in Los Angeles. Projects designed by Amphibian Arc have won numerous international competition awards and have been exhibited in the United States, Japan, Poland, and Taiwan. Amphibian Arc is currently working on "A Monument to Copernicus" in Poland, a commercial high-rise building in Shanghai, and numerous commercial and residential projects in both California and Nevada. *nonchi@arc.la.ca.us.*

Neil M. Denari. Director of SCI-ARC; After having studied at the University of Houston and received a Master of Architecture degree from Harvard University, he worked at J. S. Polshek & Partners as a senior designer for three and a half years before beginning to teach at Columbia University in 1986. He moved to Los Angeles in 1988 to begin practice as COR-TEX Architecture and, since 1998, as Neil M. Denari Architects, mixing commissions, competitions, and research projects into a larger, technical discourse about architecture. He has given more than 80 lectures worldwide about his work. *denari@sciarc.edu; http://japan.park.org/Japan/Sony/3DWorld/Neil_Denari.*

Diller + Scofidio. Both studied at the Cooper Union in New York. E. Diller presently teaches at Princeton University; R. Scofidio at Cooper Union. They collaborate on large scale mixed-media installations, projects in print, performance works and architectural works.

They have been extensively published and exhibited. Their present works in progress includes: *Facsimile*, permanent media installation, Moscone Convention Center, San Francisco; *Travelogues,* permanent media installation, JFK Airport; *Extasia, Expo 2001,* Switzerland, invited competition for exhibition grounds, in collaboration with West 8, Rotterdam; *Brasserie*, re-design of classic restaurant in the Seagram's Building, New York (originally designed by P. Johnson). *disco@interport.net.*

Winka Dubbeldam. Presently teaching at the GSAP of Columbia University in NY; she studied at The Academy of Architecture, Rotterdam, and received a Master's Degree from Columbia University. She prepared urban planning proposals as a consultant to the City Councils of Dordrecht and The Hague in Holland. Current projects of her office Archi-tectonics include a new Digital Imaging Facility in Midtown Manhattan, a mixed-use building in Brooklyn, a house in upstate NY and a proposal for three residential towers in Rotterdam (with Architektenburo Rokus Visser, Rotterdam). Her work has been widely exhibited and published in the US and Europe. She has previously worked for B. Tschumi and P. Eisenman. *wdubb4ny@bway.net; http://www.bway.net/~wdubb4ny.*

Marcos Novak. Presently teaching at UCLA in Los Angeles, and honorary co-president (with Paul Virilio) of the Transarchitectures Association in Paris. Combining elements of architecture, music, and computation, his work investigates non-Euclidean concepts of space, aspects of algorithmic emergence and morphogenesis. His designs and compositions have been realized in a variety of media and at many international venues, including television and radio programs, music and dance performances, and installations and exhibitions in the USA, Holland, Sweden, Portugal, France, Italy, Austria, Brazil, and Canada. *marcos@aud.ucla.edu; http://www.aud.ucla.edu/~marcos.*

Rashid + Couture (Asymptote Architecture). Presently teaching at the GSAP of Columbia University, H. Rashid received a Master of Architecture degree from the Cranbrook Academy of Art. L. A. Couture received her Master of Architecture degree from the Yale School of Architecture and is currently teaching at Parson's School of Design in New York. They founded Asymptote in 1987, a highly accomplished firm whose avant-garde work includes not only building designs and urban planning projects, but also gallery installations, computer-generated images and environments and multi-media digital installations. Their projects have been featured in many publications and widely exhibited in the USA and Europe. At the present they are involved in two large scale virtual architectural projects for the New York Stock Exchange and the Guggenheim Museum in New York, in addition to the Kyoto Edutainment Center in Japan. *info@asymptote-architecture.com.*

Thomas Leeser (Leeser Architecture). Presently teaching at the GSAP of Columbia University; he holds a Master of Architecture from Technische Hochschule Darmstadt, Germany. He has worked with P. Eisenman on many prestigious projects including, among others, the Wexner Center for the Visual Arts, the Columbus Convention Center, the Biocenter of J.W. Goethe University, *Choral L. Works* (Parc de la Villette) with J. Derrida. He taught a course on digital/media studios entitled *The Architecture of Navigation* at Columbia University and the University of Melbourne, Australia, followed by an exhibit which was shown at the Melbourne Arts Festival, and will soon be published in a book with the same title. Since 1989 he has been the head of Leeser Architecture, based in New York. In 1998 with other partners he founded the Bureau for Major Projects (BMP) in Melbourne, Australia. *Leeser@earthlink.net; http://www.leeser.com.*

The Information Technology Revolution in Architecture is a new series reflecting on the effects the virtual dimension is having on architects and architecture in general. Each volume will examine a single topic, highlighting the essential aspects and exploring their relevance for the architects of today.

in Architecture
Series edited by **Antonino Saggio**

Other titles in this series:

Digital Eisenman
An Office of the Electronic Era
Luca Galofaro
ISBN 3-7643-6094-1

Information Architecture
Basis and future of CAAD
Gerhard Schmitt
ISBN 3-7643-6092-5

HyperArchitecture
Spaces in the Electronic Age
Luigi Prestinenza Puglisi
ISBN 3-7643-6093-3

Virtual Terragni
CAAD in Historical and Critical Research
Mirko Galli / Claudia Mühlhoff
ISBN 3-7643-6174-3

Digital Stories
The Poetics of Communication
Maia Engeli
ISBN 3-7643-6175-1

For our free catalog please contact:

Birkhäuser – Publishers for Architecture
P. O. Box 133, CH 4010 Basel, Switzerland
Tel. ++41-(0)61-205 07 07; Fax ++41-(0)61-205 07 92
e-mail: sales@birkhauser.ch
http://www.birkhauser.ch